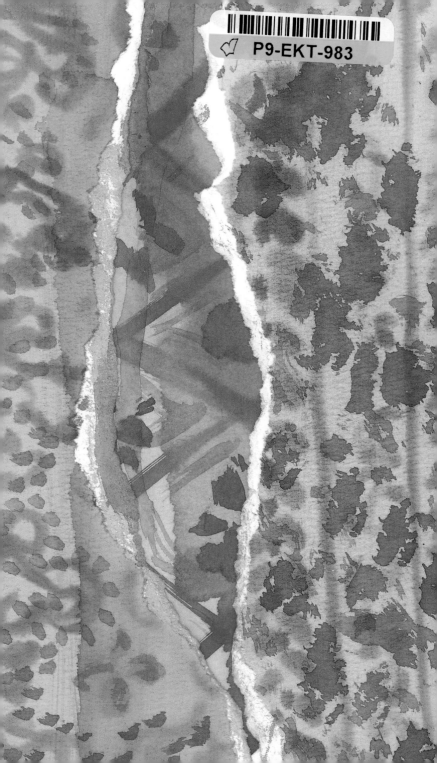

BOHEMIAN MANIFESTO

BOHEMIAN MANIFESTO

A FIELD GUIDE TO LIVING ON THE EDGE

LAREN STOVER

with PAUL GREGORY HIMMELEIN
and PATRISHA ROBERTSON

Illustrations by IZAK

BULFINCH PRESS
NEW YORK ◆ BOSTON

Bulfinch Press

Time Warner Book Group
1271 Avenue of the Americas, New York, NY 10020
Visit our Web site at www.bulfinchpress.com

First Edition
Second Printing, 2005

The author is grateful for permission to reprint the following: "1958, Paris," copyright © 2003 by Liz Dougherty Pierce; and "I am not a beat," copyright © 2004 by Ira Cohen.

Library of Congress Cataloging-in-Publication Data

Stover, Laren.
    Bohemian manifesto : a field guide to living on the edge / Laren Stover ; with Paul Gregory Himmelein and Patrisha Robertson ; illustrations by Izak — 1st ed.
        p. cm.
    Includes bibliographical references.
    ISBN 0-8212-2890-0
1. Bohemianism — United States. 2. Alternative lifestyles — United States.
3. United States — Social life and customs. I. Himmelein, Paul Gregory.
II. Robertson, Patrisha. III. Title.

HQ2044.U6S76 2004
306'.1 — dc22   2004003563

DESIGN BY DIANA HOWARD

PRINTED IN SINGAPORE

For my dads

MY BOHEMIA

A Fantasy

And so off I went, fists thrust in the torn pockets
Of a coat held together by no more than its name.
O Muse, how I served you beneath the blue;
And *oh* what dreams of dazzling love I dreamed!

My only pair of pants had a huge hole.
—Like some dreaming Tom Thumb, I sowed
Rhyme with each step. My inn was the Big Dipper.
—My stars rustled in the sky.

Roadside on warm September nights
I listened as drops of dew fell
On my forehead like fortifying wine;

And there, surrounded by streaming shadows, I rhymed
Aloud, and as if they were lyres, plucked the laces
of my wounded shoes, one foot beneath my heart.

—Arthur Rimbaud (trans. Wyatt Mason)

1958, PARIS

I beat when I play
And I play when I beat
I just want to be a round
Not a square

—PAR PIERRETTE
Liz Dougherty Pierce

CONTENTS

"The sun? The moon?
That's the question. Actually, I think I prefer the moon;
it is simpler, more noble, more primitive!"

—AGAMEMNON, late eighteenth-century painter,
Primitif precursor to the Bohemian

INTRODUCTION

To write my last book, *The Bombshell Manual of Style,* I spent two years researching Bombshells. I deconstructed their entrances, exits, tantrums, fashion statements, body language. I studied their hobbies, reading material, perfumes. I watched *How to Marry a Millionaire* at least seven times, *Promises! Promises!* at least three. If I missed any details, if I didn't recall the brand of perfume displayed near the bath, I watched the movie again. I love Bombshells. It was a joyous odyssey to study them. It was almost anthropological.

I can say, without reserve, that I am an expert on Bombshells. I've even succumbed to a few of their trappings—marabou mules, strapless satin cocktail dresses and false eyelashes on special occasions. But I am not a Bombshell.

I am a Bohemian.

This started before I was born, when I was a fetus in New York City. My parents lived in a cold-water flat on the Bowery with an

Armenian restaurant downstairs, a pull-chain toilet in the hall (shared), no sink, and mice scampering across the bare beams overhead. No bed; they slept on an extra-long sofa. The desk/dining room table was a door on metal legs. The gas stove was where the former tenant had ended it all. And there was a sociology major renting out the back room.

My Siamese-cat-adoring father was writing his dissertation at Columbia University on elitist society in Communist China and later published his first book, *The Cultural Ecology of Chinese Civilization, Peasants and Elite Society*. My mother, an actress (the Bombshell element), worked at Elizabeth Arden. Dad showered at Columbia, Mom at the salon. In an un-Bohemian maternal moment, she caved in to the idea that she needed heat and hot water for a newborn and moved back south to Baltimore.

Mom remarried. Vic DiMeo—a trumpet player who, in his New York heyday, did an arrangement for Louis Armstrong, hung with the Andrews Sisters, Nat "King" Cole, and Art Tatum, flirted with Billie Holiday at a sandwich joint between sets, played the Three Deuces with Specs Powell and Smalls' Paradise in Harlem. "We'd play a gig," he recalls, "then smoke and take a walk, and the streets were lit up with colors, neon signs, and we used to stop and watch those signs, we didn't read them, just watched them glow." In his California era, Vic studied with Darius Milhaud, played with Dave Brubeck and Paul Desmond, and had a friend named Pete who lived in a chicken coop. Composer Marty Paiche used to stop by, Vic says, and they'd all hang out at the coop and jam. Bohemianism is most glamorous in youth. Suffering for art or an ideal cloaks you in an invincible, indestructible aura of possibility. That guy in the chicken coop is a millionaire now, Vic says. Just moved to Palm Springs.

My mom and new daddy-o in their incarnation as parents were

surprisingly straitlaced. Aside from the "alternative" psychology conversations (Vic was studying psychodrama), the occasional AWOL living with us, jazz riffs on the piano, which Vic tuned himself, a nude portrait of Mom's friend Eve in their bedroom, and Sade's *Justine* lying around next to Dr. Spock, there was little to betray their Bohemian heyday. Mom did wear her water buffalo sandals in the shower to break them in, and daddy-o always dressed jazzily in thrift-shop plaids—long shorts, in say, tattersal, worn with a boxy madras shirt.

Their friends, however, made my parents look even more square. They may not have had money but they lived splendorous lives. Karl, a painter, and Zora, his wife, had a trapeze in their living room and made stilts for their wild, weedy, barefoot kids, Erik, Leif and Kiki. (Kiki is now an artist in Oregon and does lyrical paintings and murals, including a series of women breast-feeding.) Mom's friend Eve, a painter, posed nude for artists, wore Cleopatra eyeliner and taught "Tree of Life" classes. Don—he was a social worker and jazz musician—and Christine bought their old-world china at The Carry On Shop, went barefoot around the house and let Karen, my best childhood friend, go barefoot in the streets, bell-bottoms tattering and fraying along the concrete. Karen, a fellow Pisces, took me upstream to my first head shop on Howard Street; later she tuned in, "dropped out" and went on a peace caravan. Her dad dropped out, too, and for a while lived in a bus in San Francisco.

I went off to a liberal arts college, then art school in Baltimore, where I painted and etched and printed photographs and took classes at Johns Hopkins University—ancient Egyptian grammar, biosocial aspects of human sexuality, that sort of thing. I never learned how to type, balance a checkbook, do accounting, make investments, draft a legal document or sew. In my family, making a living was simply never discussed. I lacked the desire, balance and social skills to waitress, so while in art school I was a nude model for a local "charcoal club," a form of employment I fell back on while hitchhiking up the coast in California (I also did a little dancing in San Francisco to earn money for a sleeping bag) and during bouts of unemployment in New York. My *nom de nudité* was Myrrh, the name of my Abyssinian cat. To my first magazine job interview I wore a yellow thrift-shop hat and a fuchsia jacket I found in a trash can on Christopher Street. I got the job.

By the time I had been promoted to executive editor (I never got in before 11:00 a.m., so I'm not sure how that happened), I had a personal haircutter, Bohemian style. Rockets Redglare, the charming, methadone-buzzed, oversize actor from Jim Jarmusch films, used to come over with a fifth of vodka and a bottle of red wine and work his way through both as he cut my hair, then Julie's, my roommate's. The results were always asymmetrical and by the time he got to Julie, the vodka was gone and, well, you can imagine. My roommate compatibility test, by the way—I met Julie through an ad in *The Village Voice*—was to go thrift shopping with her. If she bought something, she was in. (Bingo, a plaid flannel shirt.) She was tolerant, even somewhat bemused, when I brought home a decorative plaster fox with a clock set into its side that I'd gotten for five dollars from a guy on 14th Street. My next roommate was Sara, a bass player. When she wasn't on tour we drank Beaujolais until two every morning while I painted in the living room (I was showing watercolors/collages in galleries in the East Village) and she composed on a keyboard.

I now live my own brand of Bohemian life, tinged, I admit, with some bourgeois pretense and a lot more material objects than when I first moved to New York with two chairs, a dresser, typewriter, all my paintings, some clothes and little else to a fourth-floor walk-up in Greenwich Village. Taxidermy galore, archaic appliances—a Victrola, black rotary-dial phone, same old manual typewriter, furniture and art—my own or bought or found on the streets, at flea markets or inherited—and, of course, no dishwasher or microwave. I initially cultivated these domestic eccentricities to make up for having no money. When I finally got to a point where I *could* live in a more polished, efficient, sanitized environment, I didn't want to. I still embraced my wayward nature, my untamed, serendipitous, melancholic, cluttered surroundings. Needless to say, the pet pygmy hedgehog and ferret were uncaged, my lover's idea. And when a litter of mice was born in the Victorian couch we created a cozy terrarium for them with a running wheel until it was warm enough to let them go in the spring. My apartment will never be featured in *Town & Country* or *Architectural Digest*. (Maybe *Casa Vogue,* which covers tree houses, Gypsy caravans and crumbling walls as valid ways of decorating and living. The Italians—ironically, the people who started the futurist movement—aren't afraid of peeling paint, shredded fibers, tumbling books and a few skulls lying around.)

I first had the idea of a Bohemian manual when I was working on *The Bombshell Manual.* Someone asked, "How can you do a manual for Bohemians? Aren't they always questioning everything?"

Not only questioning. Defying, rebelling, transgressing, transforming, embracing risk, excess and the idea of Utopia.

Bohemians have backbone. They're willing to suffer for their beliefs, their art. They don't sell out. They are iconoclastic, incendiary, bombastically volatile and gracefully volatile, sometimes surreal. They have poetry. The Bohemian traipses through a sky-brightening constellation of ideas, illuminating the tangled pitch-dark sky of dense, impenetrable black holes, unknown galaxies, worlds, otherworlds, underworlds. The Bohemian is drunk on words, paintings, carvings, plays, love affairs, travel, meditation, olives, cypress trees, everydayness, movie images, video images, sounds, naked flesh, all-nighters.

In my research, I ransacked the lives of the original Bohemians in Paris (chronicled by Victor Hugo, Henry Murger and Émile Zola), read poetry by Baudelaire, Apollinaire and Rimbaud, and drank up the history of absinthe. I watched Kiki de Montparnasse disrobe for artists, went caféhopping with Toulouse-Lautrec and stepped into Picasso's studio, and when I got to America, went on the road with Jack Kerouac. I read Nancy Milford's book on Edna St. Vincent Millay and reread Ginsberg's *Howl*. I delved into the lifestyle of England's first major Bohemian, Augustus John, the painter who, with his cape and earrings and costumed communal living, made Bohemianism glamorous. I took a trip over laudanum seas with Coleridge and probed the unconventional sexual mores of those Nouveau Bohemians, the Bloomsbury Group.

This book is a playful exploration. There are discourses on the three defining attributes of Bohemians: courage, audacity and revolt. There are decorating, lifestyle and fashion tips: meditations on dust (beggar's velvet; decay is emblematic of an acceptance of life and death—Bohemians feel no need to sterilize and sanitize their environment. Even my southern-belle grandmother had Bohemian leanings when it came to housekeeping, "For God's sake, don't go dusting, I won't know where anything goes," she was known to say, along with, "Leave that spider under the sink alone"), light (candles figure big here; drips are never scraped up), smoke (cigarettes, incense, pipes), asylums (always worth writing or ranting about), nudity (lots of disrobing), elixirs (absinthe, wine, coffee and more coffee), threads (poetic anarchy, deviance). But mostly it's a treatise on creativity—tapping into and releasing the Bohemian within. I recommend that everyone with a day job in a repressive corporate environment take a sabbatical. Delve into "impractical" reading that has nothing to do with getting ahead— *The Decameron,* Mallarmé, *The Secret World of the Flower Fairies* by Cicely Mary Barker (Grimms' will do, as well), books on magic mushrooms and bees. (See Reading Material.) Take a watercolor class. Sew something out of bottle green velvet or curtain material. Write an ode. Limber up by doing a drip painting. Spray-paint the edges of your Birkenstocks silver. Make a short film of yourself trying on all your clothing. Or taking off clothing. Go to Marrakech. Do something you've always wanted to (without fear), but for heaven's sake, don't take a time-management workshop.

I have deconstructed five types or classifications of Bohemians and offer examples of each. As for modern-day Bohemians, I've probed their lives, too, with fictionalized accounts of nine Bohemians. Most of the muses for these case studies are people I've known. I have altered, embellished, embroidered, created hybrids. There's a sculptor, an old-world magician, a construction worker who teaches yoga, a journalist who wears wings and an absinthe-drinking, Sufi-swirling actress named Oona. All of my characters are, as my daddy-o Vic puts it, mavericks.

Vic used to talk about working at the Chicago State Hospital, where he was a recreation therapist before getting his Ph.D. in psychology. A Bohemian himself with a lifetime of living on the edge, he knew what it was to be an outsider, an unconventional artist / thinker trying to do it his own way and yet fit in.

He never judged the patients or made any class distinction between the mentally ill and the mentally sound. "We are all the same," he always said.

Like Bohemians, the mentally ill are outlaws, upsetting the status quo with disturbing and unorthodox behavior and ideas. Vic was kind of an expert.

When a patient came up to him at the fence and said, "How do I get out of here?" Vic said, "Look, just act normal."

Tom Wolfe wrote that Bohemians are outlaws that break society's rules but want society's approval. They're just not willing to act normal. "The Bohemian is not," wrote Ada Clare, known as the "queen of Bohemia" in New York in the 1800s, "like the creature of society, a victim of rules and customs; he steps over them with an easy, graceful, joyous unconsciousness, guided by the principles of good taste and feeling."

Can and do Bohemians exist today? Can you own a DVD player and a BlackBerry Wireless and be a Bohemian? Can you have a conventional job and be a Bohemian? Yes and no. It doesn't matter what you have or don't have. What matters are ideals and maintaining creative identity. Kimberly Forrest, a *Bombshell Manual* coauthor, was writing full time at a corporate job when I met her, but in her thirty-ninth-floor office, on top of her de rigueur fashion magazines, were tipsy stacks of *The Paris Review, Granta* and *Harper's*. Everyone else was wearing institutional navy blue wool crepe suits, but she had on a hand-knit thrift-shop sweater with voluptuous flowers and brown trousers cut like gas station attendant pants from 1962. She was taking a pottery class, making tiny vessels that served no practical purpose. She condescends to write on a computer and can navigate Outlook but doesn't use air conditioning and never a hand-held device like a Palm Pilot, Walkman or cell phone; she wraps gifts in utilitarian materials—string, thread, brown paper towels, butcher paper. Her forlorn friends stop by at 3:00 a.m., and out-of-town company with children show up for a weekend and stay six months and they all share one bed. Can she function in a corporate environment and keep her individualistic integrity? Well, she decided to go freelance.

We can never re-create the unsettling, electric, unruly luster of the first Bohemians—the demimonde Bohemians, the Greenwich-Village–in-the-thirties Bohemians, the Beats or for that matter the Hippies and the Slackers. But I think it's time to be less consumed with consumerism, to get high on ideas, not things, to embrace our creativity and look inward instead of outward. To experience splendor.

AUTHOR'S DISCLAIMER: This is not a well-rounded account of Bohemian living. When a group elects to live on the edge, it's not always pretty, blissful or ecstatic. I dwell upon the originality, quirks, courage, decorative deviance and exuberance, the aspirational elements of Bohemia unclouded, for the most part, by somber depressions, morbid fantasies and extreme poverty. Just being poor doesn't make you a Bohemian.

LAREN STOVER
New York City, 2004

I
BOHEMIAN PSYCHOLOGY

DEFINING BOHEMIA

A DIAGNOSIS

"Who am I? I'm a poet. My business? Writing.
How do I live? I live.
In my happy poverty I squander like a prince,
my poems and songs of love.
In hopes and dreams and castles-in-air,
I'm a millionaire in spirit."

—RODOLFO, *La Bohème*

So, what exactly is a Bohemian? Technically, a Bohemian is a person hailing from that province of the Czech Republic or a gypsy type leading a vagabond life reading palms and tarot cards and playing strange music around the campfire with a dancing bear. The Bohemia of this book is about living beyond convention. Bohemia is an atmosphere, a way of life, a state of mind. Henry Murger, who wrote about himself and all his starving-artist friends, put the word

Bohemian into mainstream language in 1849 when his play *La Vie de Bohème* went up in Paris. He gave a label to the eccentric and socially unorthodox. Poets, painters, absinthe drinkers, dandies on the fringe—any oddball qualified.

Bohemian living or consciousness, if you will, has always been provocative. There's just something about the freedom, recklessness, scandal, artistic vision and spiritual splendor that makes it tantalizingly worthy of membership. Bohemianism is not a trend, it's a timeless movement, a way of life both fleeting and enduring that reappears every now and then as a backlash against our bourgeois, mass market, easy access culture. Bohemianism doesn't always steal the headlines. Bohemianism may be big and shocking but it may also be personal and subterranean, with quiet defiances. Bohemianism slips into our bedroom and makes a personal appearance in our dreams, sits next to us while we're in a car and whispers detours, Bohemianism is the stranger pouring stars and galaxies into our morning beverage while we watch the cat lick its paws, and it's the compulsion we have to pick up a piece of paper on the street and promise ourselves that what's written on it will be the first sentence of our next novel or the name of the yoga center or bar we're opening. Bohemianism is more than an attitude. It's the apolitical freedom of ideas, clothing and behaviors gently outside the norm. It's an elixir of undisclosed ingredients, a strange, bootleg perfume, it's the psychic, globally warmed truth serum the government wants to ban, it's the holy water of the unconscious mind, and once anointed, the underground gold mine of ideas blossoms and bleeds into the open air without self-consciousness, without reproach, without judgment.

Bohemians defy exact definition because they are essentially errant spirits. Bohemians are society's outlaws—mavericks, vagabonds, mad scientists, gypsies, theater people, artists, deviants, radicals, outsiders. They are, in essence, all one clan.

Bohemians transform, mutating and evolving from Dandy to Beat to Flower Child per the prevailing zeitgeist.

You know them when you see them:

She wears velvet in the rain.

He dances with pigeons and does magic tricks in the bookstore café.

They walk from Nice to Florence and have a child named Sienna.

They drive a school bus, despite the parking challenges . . . and eat porridge while drinking Languedoc.

They wear contrarianism more liberally than ordinary mortals wear polyester.

You see them selling hand-knit hats to tourists on the streets of SoHo, heading to Veselka coffee shop in the East Village at noon for a morning coffee, wearing Value Village as if it were Yohji Yamamoto, reading Gertrude Stein, dressed like George Sand at cafés in the Butte aux Cailles, safe from tourist buses since it's in the thirteenth arrondissement, listening to jazz at Les Instants Chavirés in Paris, hiking in a fedora in Katmandu, doing performance art in Williamsburg, moving into a new space in the Tenderloin district in San Francisco because they find North Beach too cliché, on their third pint at a tavern talking about the creation of the universe and the six months they spent in the rain forest and the miracle drug they found growing at the roots of a particular type of tree and by the way it gets you high, sipping free wine in plastic cups at art galleries as artist, collector and muse, reading poetry in bookstores in Berlin, modeling for nude photographs in a cemetery in Prague and scavenging junk shops by bus for vintage furniture later sold to antique dealers to keep themselves in absinthe.

Bohemians may get on your nerves, but even when they appear to be idle, down-and-out, opinionated Slackers, they're stirring things up. Bohemians are the ultimate elitists. They want to run things. They break the rules, set the trends, knit the knits, destroy the art and reinvent the art that everyone wants, or will want. Bohemians start movements. Bohemians change thinking. Bohemians stay up all night talking, and sometimes they write manifestos. Bohemians cross cultures and integrate mantras, philosophies, substances and clothing seamlessly into everyday life. Bohemians tenderly and violently create new work and change paradigms. Bohemians change the world.

BOHEMIAN RHAPSODIES

A TREATISE on BOHEMIAN CONSCIOUSNESS

The Bohemian is not a follower of the virtues espoused by bourgeois society: routine, temperance, convention, mediocrity, materialism (unless they are Dandies) and respectability. Bohemians despise authority, the status quo and, because they are often broke, capitalism and consumerism.

The Bohemian makes do—creatively, exultantly—and does not need the newest appliance, car or gadget to impress, to feel whole, to define himself or herself, to pursue dreams.

The true Bohemian is a connoisseur of texture, color and sensation. While the bourgeoisie can experience excitement, a feeling of fulfillment only through consuming, the Bohemian is exhilarated by observation, by creation, by experience itself.

Shopping doesn't ignite poetry. It is believed that romantic, lucid, nocturnal observations of frost upon a window (not laudanum in this case) inspired Samuel Taylor Coleridge to write "Frost at Midnight" (the title suggests the writer is not an early-to-bed type).

Bohemians do not take comfort in consuming to fill the hollow emptiness of existence that rattles like small shattered bones; they find poetry in the free and everyday things: the pinked and silvered light of Paris in early October, a spiderweb decked out in jewel-like dew, a nineteenth-century china tea set in an antique shop window next to a taxidermy fox, humble objects and books and paintings and conversations in a coffee shop, things overheard in a botanical garden or on a wharf. The Bohemian takes comfort in creating poetry, whether it is poems or plays or music or oil paintings or pottery or knittery or movies or magic or creating patterns and coziness by throwing a few shawls or rugs over a couch or chair. The Bohemian delights in the way light changes in the room when a gold embroidered sari, picked up on a trip to India, is draped over the lamp. The Bohemian sees enchantment and possibility everywhere. If a Bohemian is ever bored by quotidian existence, remedies include absinthe, composing a manifesto or splitting town.

The Bohemian reuses, recycles, reinvents, drapes, reconstructs, transforms, creates. An old, moth-eaten cashmere sweater is an opportunity not to shop for a new one but to add fancy stitchwork in a contrasting color.

It is splendor in which the Bohemian lives, not squalor—the splendor of the creative mind—and it requires ingenuity, freethinking and nerve. (For the Bohemian, beauty exists in suffering as much as in pleasure.)

Bohemians are just as interested in creating ambience, an effect, as bourgeois society is, but they do not need a bankroll to accomplish it or a magazine to show them how. Corporate culture holds no sway over them. While they may have proletarian ideals, they do not want to take orders; their idea of hard labor is selling poetry, pottery, plays, music, photographs—even themselves when they model nude for art classes or artists. A Bohemian would rather pose in an uncomfortable position for hours and days, even weeks, to be immortalized as Leda with the swan and contribute to a creative endeavor, than have a steady position typing someone else's correspondence and keeping track of their appointments. As the avant-garde poet and artist Mina Loy said of her daughter Joella, "No child of mine will ever be a secretary." She furthermore forbade her daughter to become a teacher, a position that was, in her mind, bourgeois. Respectability is never a concern.

Bohemians rarely have regular jobs. They are contemptuous of nine-to-five. When they do have jobs, it's not for long. This is because they sketch, work on novels (annoyingly, the place, unless an insane asylum, is never interesting enough to write about), use office equipment to make flyers for their performances and gigs and read books.[1] William Burroughs wrote to Allen Ginsberg: "A regular job drains one's very lifeblood. It's supposed to. They want everything you've got." [2]

In addition to mental hospital orderly, Bohemian jobs run the gamut from editing literary magazines, freelance set designing and window display, to photographing artwork, pressing wheatgrass in a juice bar and hand-painting neckties. Bohemians would rather be a night guard in a cemetery where they can read, write music or work on a novel (as long as there's no surveillance camera) than a financial analyst.

1.   "I was fired one day because I was caught typing out from Nietzsche's *Anti-Christ* while working on work time until the big vice-president came through and saw me—fired." Henry Miller.

2.   The Bohemian disdain for jobs goes back much further than the fifties and even Mina Loy's Paris in the twenties. In her book *The Bohemians, La Vie de Bohème in Paris 1830–1914*, Joanna Richardson writes, "Some [Bohemians] resolutely refused to compromise with the bourgeois need to earn a living: they considered it undignified, and an admission of failure."

Unresourceful, un-trust-funded Bohemians lacking brilliance or recognition didn't seem to live very long in nineteenth-century Paris, but a well-written obituary could romanticize a tragic, short life, perpetuating the dangerously glittering Bohemian lifestyle:

"There is in Paris a multitude of young artists, full of resolution and hope. They scorn the realities of life and they ask nothing of the world but glory. A studio in some attic or other, a few reliefs and engravings, a skeleton, a little paint, a canvas and some brushes, that's all their fortune. Often they even lack bread, but they have the world of the imagination, and this world is very rich. There is nothing venal in their natures, and so they are called eccentric. . . . They are not concerned with politics . . . but if a coup d'état should come, they are the first man to the barricades. . . . My poor friend Charles Bécoeur was one of these. He was twenty-four. Painting had been his one ambition since he was a child. He had given it the whole of his young life. . . ."

(*The Bohemians,* Joanna Richardson)

Bohemians never sacrifice art for respectability and state-of-the-art comforts. The driving force of consumerist culture declares tacitly, *You are incomplete if you don't own this.*[3]

They are downright disdainful of capitalism and its ever-tightening noose and prefer, when they do consume, to support independent, small establishments. Even Bohemians with trust funds have an egalitarian streak. Think French Revolution: *Liberté, Égalité, Fraternité.*

Bohemians are disdainful of the status quo. If short hair is the norm, they will grow it long. When long hair is in vogue, they get out the razor.

Bohemians are counterculture. They embrace counterculture ideals. They create and indulge in work that goes against the grain. Bohemians admire radical art, writing, fashion and thinking—until it becomes mainstream. They are always ahead of the curve, showcasing their transgressive, explosive, unsettling and deviant work in alternative journals and with small presses, in small galleries, in experimental theaters and cafés in fringe neighborhoods. Frontier neighborhoods become

3.   The Rolling Stones illuminated the evil persuasiveness of consumerism with their song "Satisfaction."

up-and-coming only after Bohemians have brought in their art, per-formances, readings, dance, bars and handmade clothing, candle, jewelry and leather shops. The Bohemian can always sniff out any-thing "alternative" that has become mainstream and is soon on to a more subtle underground Bohemia, new alternatives that outclass the mass-marketed "fringe."

When Starbucks and the Gap move in, the Bohemian moves out. Or gets kicked out.

Courage

Giving up security takes guts. Bohemians have the courage to reject mainstream society; to follow an ideal and forsake praise and security; to alienate family; to be, as Jack Kerouac put it, "yourself at whatever cost."

Bohemians have the moral courage to wrestle with self-doubt, take risks, revolutionize, dismantle and shock, endure criticism and rejection. Bohemians wittingly and passionately engage in behaviors that may yield no financial gain. They have the courage to embrace estrangement, controversy and poverty. This may mean being cut off from the family fortune or leaving a lucrative career. Baudelaire's *Les Fleurs du Mal* created such a scandal that his family withdrew and left him to wallow in debt. When André Breton refused to cease his Dada activities and return to law school, his family pulled the plug on his finances. Gauguin gave up a career in banking to move to Tahiti to commune with nature and paint partially clad women.

Work created by Bohemians is routinely ostracized. In 1948, Antonin Artaud's play *To Have Done with the Judgment of God,* commissioned by French radio, was banned on the eve that it was supposed to broadcast for being undecipherable, obscene and unintelligible. Some Bohemian work is never aired or published or exhibited at all. Bohemians desire celebrity in their lifetime but will settle for fame and recognition after death.

Bohemians have the courage to undergo exile, sentenced or self-imposed. Exiled Bohemians include Voltaire, Zola, Courbet and Polanski, to name a few.

Bohemians have the courage to rush in where the bourgeois fear to tread, pioneering borderline sections of town, squatting in abandoned buildings and setting up camp on the wrong side of the tracks.

Audacity

Bohemians have pluck. The nerve to flaunt unfavorable and intrepid ideas and creations. The confidence to champion unpopular causes, to disregard decorum and morality, to be transgressive.

Auntie Mame, the starring character of the 1955 novel (the 1958 film is a Bohemian must-see), epitomizes the Nouveau Bohemian. Always more interested in shock value and exploring alternatives than respectability, Auntie Mame defies convention glamorously; she's audacity with a little sugar on top. She sends her nephew to an all-nude school in Greenwich Village and hosts colorful, unconventional cocktail parties with over-the-top decorations.

Jackson Pollock qualifies. It took courage to leave New York City and set up a studio in rural Long Island[4] but audacity to bypass the brush and drip paint from a stick. And audacity is the word to describe his behavior the night he took off his clothes and urinated in the fireplace at a swank party at Peggy Guggenheim's house.

The surrealists were perpetually audacious. It takes audacity to make a teacup of fur or display a urinal as art.

Andrés Serrano fits the bill with his controversial photograph "Piss Christ." Bohemians find nothing abhorrent in bodily functions and delight in shocking others who do. (See Art.)

The Italian futurists, led by F. T. Marinetti with his *Futurist Manifesto* in 1909, virtually defined audacity. It takes audacity to create a manifesto that would "deliver Italy from its gangrene of professors, archaeologists, tourist guides and antiquaries," to desire the destruction of museums and libraries.

---

4. The Hamptons stopped being Bohemian in the 1950s. Most serious Bohemians will not even accept a free weekend there.

Émile Zola and Norman Mailer both had the audacity to come to the aid of the accused and the incarcerated.[5]

Convicted killer Jack Henry Abbott, an inmate serving a maximum sentence of nineteen years for murder (not a Bohemian but certainly a revolutionary type), wrote to Norman Mailer to offer his insights. Rooted in Bohemian idealism and familiar with violence sprung from passion, Mailer was moved by Abbott's "vision of more elevated human relations" and his revolutionary discourses on Mao and Stalin. Mailer had the audacity to think he could help free him. And he did. Along with an editor from Random House, Mailer convinced the Utah Board of Corrections of Abbott's literary talent. A book was in the works.

Abbott set a good example. For a month. But he was a loose cannon and he went off. Murdered again. Bohemians can never see this coming. They always vote for the underdog, the person or group oppressed by the "system."

Boundaries, rules and laws are easily blurred and broken by the Bohemian who can justify many acts in the name of art.

Émile Zola championed the cause of scapegoat Captain Dreyfus (imprisoned on bogus espionage and treason charges) and later wrote *J'accuse!,* an open letter to the French president attacking the conservative forces in France. Zola was forced to flee.

Bohemian audacity prompts people to say: Just who does he think he is?

---

5.   This may be, in part, empathy, as Bohemians are often incarcerated themselves. This applies to William Burroughs, Jack Kerouac, Lenny Bruce, Oscar Wilde, Abbie Hoffman, Jean Genet, Paul Verlaine, Keith Richards and Keith Moon, to name a few.

Revolt

Revolt comes naturally to Bohemians; they are contrary, irreverent and disobedient. They like to shake things up. They tickle, rattle, inspire, amuse, repulse and overthrow.

Bohemians revolt against dress codes, the circadian clock, business hours, temperance, established mores, the conventional idea of a work ethic, established art forms, politics, traditional living arrangements and institutions. (Exception: mental institutions; see Asylum—Home Away from Home.)

Bohemians are powder kegs looking for a match. They're all about rebellion, and they always have a cause. Even if their cause is misguided, the Bohemian has a purpose, an ideology, a poetic or anarchical vision unaffected by conventional views.

Bohemians see all rules and most laws as an infringement of their personal and artistic freedom. This may bring celebrity, infamy or assassination. The Bohemian sees insurrection not as an act of revolt but rather as an act of transformation. Revolt, after all, is always a catalyst for change.

Revolution, to the Bohemian, may be artistic.

Matisse and other painters upset the French Academy by using bold, emotional brushwork and color. The critics slapped the label *fauve* or "wild beast" on them for their blatant disregard of traditional painting.

Revolution may be political.

The French revolutionary Jean-Paul Marat and Che Guevara both helped topple oppressive/imperialist regimes. This naturally led to their assassinations.

Or revolution may be expressed by something as simple as letting goats run loose in the house (see Wildlife) or starting a meal with dessert. Bohemians lead, but by default. They depart from the norm and eventually, usually after it's too late, gain acceptance.

Bohemians have a violent contempt for rules, yet they can't resist composing manifestos: *The Futurist Manifesto, The Communist Manifesto, Bauhaus Manifesto, The Theater of Cruelty* (First Manifesto, 1932, Second Manifesto, 1933), Guillaume Apollinaire's manifesto, *L'Esprit nouveau et les Poètes, The Surrealist Manifesto* and of course the two manifestos by the artist Ultra Violet, muse to both Salvador Dalí and Andy Warhol.

Manifestos are revolutionary—they are, in essence, rules on how to break rules, to see everything in a new light. They do not have to be of a grandiose nature. Rules may, in fact, be quite personal. The Viennese writer Peter Altenberg (a fixture at Café Central) drew up a set of rules for people who wanted to join him at the café. "Rules for My Reserved Table" forbade nail grooming— "clipped nails can easily fly into beer glasses"—as well as the use of certain words and discussion of certain topics. There were repercussions for breaking these rules; transgressors had to fork over cash—the sums varying by offense—or buy a bottle of Champagne.

BOHEMIAN BON MOTS

"God thinks in the genius, dreams in the poets and sleeps in the rest of humanity."

—PETER ALTENBERG

"I don't know how to drive, just typewrite."

—JACK KEROUAC

"The life of the young artist here is the easiest, merriest, dirtiest existence possible."

—WILLIAM MAKEPEACE THACKERAY

"Art washes away from the soul the dust of everyday life."

—PABLO PICASSO

"Houses are full of things that gather dust."

—JACK KEROUAC

"Travel, leave everything, copy the birds. The home is one of civilization's sadnesses. In a few years humanity will go back to its nomadic state."

—GUSTAVE FLAUBERT

"It was ecstasy sleeping on the sidewalk of Washington Square, realizing I had no commitments to anything or anyone."

—MARLON BRANDO in his 1994 memoir *Songs My Mother Taught Me*

"The books we need are the kind that act upon us like a misfortune, that make us suffer like the death of someone we love more than ourselves, that make us feel as though we were on the verge of suicide, or lost in a forest remote from all human habitation—a book should serve as the ax for the frozen sea within us."

—from a letter of FRANZ KAFKA to OSKAR POLLAK

"Trees pass information on how to hold up hillsides and how to grow, and they also know how to communicate feelings."

—JULIA BUTTERFLY HILL

"If it hadn't been for the beats, America wouldn't have known about Zen, wouldn't have known about Buddhism."

—RAY MANZAREK, The Doors

"In art there is either plagiarism or revolution."

—PAUL GAUGUIN

"To be successful painting has to be unsaleable."

—MAN RAY

"If someone tells you not to do something—that's a clue to do it."

—MARK INNERST

"I wish I could live like a poor man, but with a lot of money."

—PABLO PICASSO

"Poetry is the language of a state of crisis."

—STÉPHANE MALLARMÉ

"Good taste is the enemy of creativity."

—PABLO PICASSO

"Beauty exists only in struggle."

—*The Futurist Manifesto*, F. T. MARINETTI

"I don't think there is any truth. I think there are only points of view."

—ALLEN GINSBERG

"Talk! If you can't think of anything to say, tell a lie!"

—AUGUSTUS JOHN

"I am surrealism."

—SALVADOR DALÍ

"God is really another painter . . . like me."

—PABLO PICASSO

"What we see isn't in things, but in our souls."

—SALVADOR DALÍ

"Poetry, after all, is the feast which life offers those who know how to receive with their eyes and hearts, and understand."

—LE CORBUSIER

"I've always thought that describing dreams is very boring and talking about hallucinations is, too. The important thing is to provoke them, and to provoke them without drugs, which is what I do. I paint pictures that really produce . . . hallucinations."

—SALVADOR DALÍ

"I hate to advocate drugs or liquor, violence, insanity, but in my case, it's worked."

—HUNTER S. THOMPSON

"Thanks to the hashish I was able to sketch an authentic goblin. Up to now I had only heard them moaning and moving at night in my cupboard."

—THÈOPHILE GAUTIER

"Life's a banquet and most poor suckers are starving to death!"

—AUNTIE MAME

"I'm not afraid of computers taking over the world. They're just sitting there. I can hit them with a two-by-four."

—THOM YORKE

"Whatever the reasons, I enjoyed being nude; it felt natural to me. I got the same kind of pleasure from being free of clothing that many people get from being well dressed."

—CHARIS WILSON (Edward Weston's most famous nude model)

"I will go to the bank by the wood and become undisguised and naked."

—WALT WHITMAN

"*La Bohème* was the *Sex and the City* of the 1800s."

—Baz Luhrmann

"Drink to me."

—last words of Pablo Picasso

II

BOHEMIAN
IDENTIFICATION

BOHEMIAN BREAKDOWN

No one can truly define a Bohemian, although Bohemians themselves, from Charles Baudelaire to Jack Kerouac, have tried to name and justify their particular brand.[1]

Jack Kerouac defined his type as Beat in 1948 when he and writer John Clellon Holmes were contemplating the meaning of the Lost Generation and the subsequent existentialism and he said, "You know, this is really a beat generation." Baudelaire was one of the first Bohemians to identify with the Dandy and carried on extensively to define the outlaw sensibility of this type.

That said, there are, if you use a little imagination, five distinct Bohemian mind-set/styles: the Nouveau Bohemian, the Gypsy Bohemian, the Beat Bohemian, the Zen Bohemian and the Dandy Bohemian.

1. Bohemians conversely may protest stereotypes and define themselves through poetry. Please refer to Ira Cohen's poem.

There are also many crossovers and hybrids. Beats, for example, may have Zen leanings or the foppish trappings of a Dandy. The Bohemian by nature is not easily classified like species of birds.

I am not a beat
though I have performed
with them all etc.
I am an electronic
multimedia Shaman,
a Naga Hipster, an Akashic Agent, an Outlaw of the Spirit
I am the One out of
a Hundred
I am the Bearded Iris, the flower of chivalry
with a sword for a leaf
& a lily for a heart
I am the Rainbow—a hybrid of celestial

                              hues

blue in the end, a message between

                       Gods.

I am your shadow in the

               darkness,

your reflection in the

           mirror

I am the Jack in your box.

—Ira Cohen

The Nouveau Bohemian

The Nouveau Bohemian brings elements of traditional Bohemian ideology into harmony with contemporary culture without losing sight of the basic tenets—the glamour, the art, the nonconformity. And while Nouveaus may suffer poetically, artistically and romantically, they have what appears to be, at first, one advantage over other Bohemians—the Nouveau has money.

The Nouveau Bohemian is not to be confused with the bourgeois Bohemian. While "only a shallow person would spend hundreds of dollars on caviar, but a deep person would gladly shell out that much for top-of-the-line mulch," according to the definitive bourgeois Bohemian guide, *Bobos in Paradise,* Nouveau Bohemians, like the poverty-stricken characters in Henry Murger's book *Scènes de la Bohème* (popularized by Puccini's opera *La Bohème,* now a musical) who get a little money and spend it all in one night, celebrate extravagance, art and deviance. The Nouveau Bohemian does not consider the Bobo, who carefully distinguishes between need and want, to be a Bohemian at all. Bohemians are not shopping at stores that sell make-believe old things and mass-market dinnerware. Ostentation is not a disgrace to the Nouveau or to any Bohemian who gladly spends it when they have it; the bottom line is not things but ideas: freedom of the spirit, extravagance of the spirit, *that* is the requisite.

Therefore, money or a trust fund does not exclude those wishing to embrace Bohemian life.[2] In fact, a trust fund allows for the pursuit of art unencumbered by work, particularly nine-to-five, to which the Bohemian is ill suited. J. K. Huysmans explores this in his decadent *fin-de-siècle* novel, *Au Rebours,* or *Against the Grain,* which perfectly encapsulates the Bohemian spirit of an aristocrat. The pursuit of money is never violently important to the Bohemian, and not having to pursue it would seem, at first, an ideal situation. Champagne, fine wine, Pernod, poetry—time to read and write it—opera, theater, the Nouveau Bohemian can have it all. However, as the element of struggle is virtually removed by an income provided without work, dilettantism is a danger. It is with the greatest diligence and raw passion that Nouveau Bohemians must apply themselves so as to create an unconventional charm, mien and lifestyle. Aspiring to Bohemia requires a commitment, and the Nouveau Bohemian is wise to make acquaintance with poverty-ridden counterparts to kindle the underlying deviance that cannot be mimicked by style alone.

The Nouveau Bohemian hosts parties of the most extravagant sort. Artists may paint special murals just for the event, furniture may be designed, and engraved invitations tied to peacock feathers may be sent by messenger. Nothing is out of the question. The Nouveau may also be of the squandering, dissolute sort with a loathing of labor and love of pleasure and excess.

2. "Gabriel Guillemot, in 1868, made clear that Bohemia—defined in his way [as 'all those whose existence is a problem, all those who live by expedients']— had no essential tie with the condition of poverty that a Murger or a Privat had assumed was natural to it. There were Bohemians at every social level . . . whoever built his or her existence on a show of wealth, position, knowledge, or talent that was in fact the product of pretence or illusion was a Bohemian." (*Bohemian Paris* by Jerrold Seigel)

Altruism with the funds to back it is one of the most positive attributes of the Nouveau Bohemian. The Nouveau may be on the board of directors of an animal shelter or rescue. Nouveaus help with fund-raising and are living proof that rescued animals make good pets. The Nouveau may take in a large, abandoned, mangy dog that becomes absolutely gentle and devoted in addition to growing back a lustrous coat. Once rescued from the "pound," the floppy-eared rabbit that has tired of being poked by preschoolers and has begun to bite becomes a cuddly companion.

A Nouveau Bohemian heiress may be an expatriate for a while and live in a villa built for the Medici before moving to New York, where she will support anarchists and socialists and hold salons for Bohemians who want to give society, art and literature a makeover. Fringe theater in particular is of interest to Nouveaus, although they may dabble in all of the arts.

Or the Nouveau Bohemian may go all the way and fall for a starving artist. The Nouveau who is, say, a successful model in New York City may then spend weekends with the new lover who is living in and restoring a nineteenth-century house in Pennsylvania that was previously owned by a Mennonite—no electricity, no running water, just a little creek over the hill, and an outhouse in the back. The former model will find this charming, like playing in a primitive life-size dollhouse, at least in the summer and fall, and will go to country auctions with the artist. Best of all, the Nouveau is a muse for the artist. This way, his or her modeling career need not come to an end.

The Gypsy Bohemian

These are the expatriate types. They create their own Gypsy nirvana wherever they go. They are folksy flower children, hippies, psychedelic travelers, fairy folk, dreamers, Deadheads, Phish fans, medievalists, anachronistic throwbacks to a more romantic time. They may listen to Joan Baez, Marianne Faithfull, early Bob Dylan, Joni Mitchell and Captain Beefheart but more than likely they make their own music, even if it's playing the spoons.

Gypsies scatter like seeds on the wind, don't own a watch, show up on your doorstep and disappear in the night. They're happy to sleep in your barn and may have without you even knowing it. They are comfortable living out of cars and vans and are nondigital. The only time line they can rely on is the one on your palm, which they will undoubtedly read, either that or they'll cast your chart, tell your fortune or do your numbers. Gypsies like jobs that they can pack up in a bag, or not pack at all. They are painters (canvases and houses), muralists (the ones with a baby strapped to them while they paint), sign painters for small establishments, dancers, singers, actors and musicians. Other Gypsy jobs include juggling, carpentry, leather tooling, jewelry making and midwifery.

Gypsies also give lessons: music, singing, dance, especially tango and belly dancing, painting, sculpting, welding, language, horseback riding, fencing and stage combat. When they set their mind to it they get extra work in films and an occasional theater piece. They play Gypsy, tango, chamber and medieval and Celtic music for parties and weddings, and of course they play on the street.

They know a little about a lot of things, like how to milk a goat and what to feed a wild abandoned baby animal, how to fix a carnival ride, make candles and soap.

It is not wise to play cards with them.

Gypsies wear the traditional clothing of their native country when it's considered quaint and out of style and embrace their lost heritages. They will also embrace a new heritage. They costume themselves after lost cultures and forgotten times. They practice crafts on the verge of extinction: stone carving and masonry, glassblowing, papermaking, paper marbling, stained glass, frescos and encaustic. They hand make their own violins, mandolins and dulcimers. They love pocket instruments and play the pennywhistle, recorder, Jew's harp and kazoo. The largest thing they own, besides their vehicle, may be a harp or potter's wheel. They'd rather tell stories than read them.

Their books will be *Beowulf, The Tale of Genji,* Grimms' fairy tales, *Dracula,* poetry by Robert Burns and Sir Walter Scott, *The Sibyl* by Pär Lagerkvist, *Till We Have Faces* by C. S. Lewis, biographies of Augustus John and small leather-bound books with faded covers and crumbling tea-colored pages that are at least a hundred years old. Never magazines or newspapers, except for the classifieds.

They make wind chimes out of old silverware or broken pottery. Mix their own essential oils, grow their own herbs, embroider their clothing, crochet their own clothing, build little houses in old tree stumps for elves. They may even decide to settle down later in life and form a commune with other like-minded Bohemians.

Here they will keep goats and sheep and make yogurt and cheese. They will keep bees and sell honey. Their children will be tutored at home and on the road and run around naked and free. Good luck trying to figure out the family tree.

The Beat Bohemian

Reckless, raggedy, rambling, drifting, down-and-out, Utopia-seeking. It might look like Beats suffer for their ideals, but they've let go of material desire. As Jack Kerouac put it, "If you own a rug, you own too much."

Beats are free spirits. They believe in freedom of expression. They travel light, but there's always a book or a notebook in their pocket. Beats are not picky about where they sleep, and they're not too picky about who they sleep with, either. Beats are uninhibited and are always taking off their clothes. This will be for spiritual reasons, such as expressing "spiritual nakedness" at a poetry reading, or pornographic reasons, but only if they need the money.

Beats take writing seriously and quote Baudelaire when they have a fever, Keats during courtship and Walt Whitman when making love.[3] They save the lines from Tennessee Williams' *The Fugitive*

3.   Allen Ginsberg recites Whitman during an intimate act in Diane di Prima's *Memoirs of a Beatnik*.

Kind for the night before they take off again, the part about the bird that has no legs and spends all of its life on the wing, sleeping on the wind.

Beats dabble in Zen and add hijinx to their yoga practice, like trying to make love in the Tibetan yabyum or lotus position. The Beats are the ones who have read *The Kama Sutra* and have tried out most of the positions, but don't remember too much because they were inebriated, though they're pretty sure about the ones they wrote about in their notebook afterward.

They write unsaleable, unpublishable manuscripts that are later published, censored, banned and burned, and they make dreamlike, plot-free movies and documentaries on house cats, ecstatic voodoo rituals and sacred, madcap celebrations. Beats choreograph vivid and provocative dances and make art that is all about drips, spontaneity and the act of creation itself. Beats thrive on movement, which is why the road has a near mystical appeal to them. They build worlds out of their unhardened hearts and intoxicated souls, and they are more interested in recording their truths and self-expression than making a sale, not that they don't try, and sometimes it's a friend who tries for them.

Beats jam, improvise, extemporize, blow ethereal notes into the universe, write poetry, ramble and wreck cars. They live on the edge of ideas. They take the part and then make up their own lines. They have conversations with constellations, chant Om Shanti on talk shows and see the sacred in all life, from nature to hobos. Beats express themselves without censor and are pretty much up for anything. A nocturnal drive to New Orleans, stopping only for food, fuel and smokes, a threesome or foursome in Tangier, a week-long bender in Mexico. They'll go anywhere at the drop of a hat or beret, with only the clothes on their back. They'll worry about the details later: sleeping arrangements, food, cash. Actually, they won't worry about details, which is why things always seem to work out except for those glitches, sleepovers in jail. They've taken a tip from the Zen Bohemian: no expectations, no disappointments. And they never worry about grooming or hygiene. Communion with the road and heeding the howl of poetry is much more important than a shower. Besides, they know they'll eventually cross paths with a body of water—lake, fountain, ocean or sink.

The Zen Bohemian

No other Bohemians fathom the transient, green and meditative quality of life better than the Zens, even if they're in a rock band, which they often are. The Zen is post-Beat, a Bohemian whose quest has evolved from the artistic, smoky, literary and spiritually wanderlustful to the spiritually lustful.

Zens are more into astral traveling than asphalt traveling and also go out on a spiritual limb: organic farms, organic weed, no weed, mantras, yoga mats, hatha yoga, kundalini yoga, every kind of yoga, ashrams, gurus, cosmic music, songs of the whales, songs of the dolphins, saving the whales, saving the dolphins, chants, Indian Vedic music, world music, tantric sex, chakra healing, shiatsu, acupuncture, tai chi, qigong, meditation, Tibetan bells. Zens realize the body only goes so far and that you can't take a Rolex or

Lamborghini with you, not that they'll own either of those things, or even any watch. Zens are curious about whether it's possible to spontaneously smell sandalwood after a deep meditation and care about the well-being of manatees and coral reefs and rain forests. Zens protest nuclear power and are all for solar energy, even if their only personal exposure to it was their dad's pocket calculator. They are the ones sending all those petition and activist emails:

Like,

Say no to HR 2693 and prevent weakening of Marine Mammal Protection Act.

Or,

Hi, all—Here is a great little piece by Krugman that, as it reviews two new books, neatly encapsulates many key topical points about how the current government has succeeded in so many questionable enterprises—and how the public's complacency has enabled this course of events. . . .

Zens, like Beats and Gypsy or Hippie Bohemians, are never chosen for jury duty on criminal court cases because they believe drugs should be legal, even if they are not users. Rather a wholesome lot, they're prone toward the more natural drug forms and rarely use drugs created in a lab, which might, as author Tom Robbins puts it facetiously, "crack their aura." They tend to grow their own pot and wormwood and even try their hand at poppies. They may dabble in hashish, salvia, peyote and opium. In addition to reading haiku—minute landscapes that give a glimpse into a universal consciousness and the big picture—the Zen delves into reading material that reinforces nature longings, archaic ritual and time and space travel, like poetry by Zen Beat Gary Snyder, *The Book of Tea, The Dharma Bums, The Time Machine, A Brief History of Time, Chaos, String Theory* and Carlos Castaneda's *Journey to Ixtlan*. A typical Zen pickup line, borrowed from something Don Juan says to Castaneda: "Think of your death now. It is at arm's length. It may tap you any moment, so really you have no time for crappy thoughts and moods." This only works on other Zens.

Zens have read Nick Tosches' article on opium in *Vanity Fair,* which reinforces their desire to try the stuff someday, and of course they have read the laudanum-inspired poetry of Samuel Taylor Coleridge, ditto.

Zens make trips to India, Japan, Peru, New Zealand or Tibet. Zens learn Sanskrit, weave, knit, paint spirits and oceans and landscapes, create their own cosmic greeting cards, make their own paper, pottery, prayer beads and jewelry inspired by travels, by words found in antique dictionaries from flea markets. They favor beads and the lost wax method for jewelry making and know the power and significance of crystals and stones.

Like Gypsy Bohemians, Zens raise llamas, goats and sheep and pick mushrooms. If they eat granola they make their own and use rice or oat milk if they are vegans. Seaweed of all varieties and miso soup are staples in the Zen diet.

Zens read ingredients and boycott products tested on animals and anything containing formaldehyde, toluene or sodium lauryl sulfate, among other chemicals, even though this means not wearing nail polish and using shampoo that doesn't foam.

Zen hobbies include surfing (the Internet and ocean), snowboarding and hiking.

Typical jobs and/or studies of the Zen include: alternative healing, iridology, Sanskrit, yoga, oceanography, eco-warrior, astronomy, organic farming, juicing at health food stores, graphic design, software design, massage therapy, Reiki, architecture—no skyscrapers—working for Greenpeace, Peace Corps, sound engineer, documentary filmmaker (goes for all Bohemians) and, most popular, musicians. They may play flute, bongos or the didgeridoo.

The Dandy Bohemian

A little seedy, a little haughty, slightly shredded or threadbare, Dandies are the most polished of all Bohemians even when their clothes are tattered. The Dandy aspires to old money without the money. They refuse to get with the program. They might wear only vintage clothing found in flea markets and refuse to own modern conveniences. They prefer engraved calling cards to telephones, and when they do own a phone they insist upon a rotary, preferably in black. You are more likely to find unpopular liqueurs such as Chartreuse and Earl Grey brandy in the Dandy home than a six-pack of Budweiser. In fact, you will never find a six-pack in the Dandy's quarters, though Alsatian ale is a possibility, and this will have a cork. This does not mean that the Dandy refuses Budweiser at a picnic. That would be impolite.

The Dandy laments that the values of honor, elegance and dignity have fallen by the wayside along with starched collars and/or ruffled cuffs. They ignore the world of baseball caps and T-shirts with corporate logos, and reality TV. They resist global marketing and refuse to be robbed of their individuality. Dandy Bohemians are anachronistic, re-creating archaic fashions, lifestyles and manners. Dandyism isn't just about an excessive love of material elegance, however. As Charles Baudelaire acknowledged, Dandies are looking for distinction as well as lost values, and they best distinguish themselves through dress. The Dandy has never been interested in being "natural."

While Dandies might be thrifty by circumstance, they abhor frugality and embrace excess in clothing, beverages, food and their *objets d'art*. Should you meet a Dandy Bohemian or visit a Dandy's apartment you will immediately think of an aristocrat who has fallen on hard times—part Oscar Wilde, part *Addams Family,* a little *Scarlet Pimpernel.* Dandies dream of having a manservant, handmaiden and chauffeur.

The Dandy Bohemian goes in for lawn sports—healthy competition is fine as long as no sweating is involved. Croquet and badminton are favorites. So is anything that can be played while holding on to a martini or cigarette holder, e.g., shuffleboard and billiards (never pool), chess, cards and the roulette wheel. It is not uncommon for a Dandy in a long silk bathrobe to be spotted through the hedges around noon playing a game of croquet. Tennis is too strenuous and the costume appalling. The more adventurous Dandy, however, may fence. If so, the Dandy prefers the foil and épée to the saber.

Dandies are fastidious when it comes to accoutrements. They would never be caught using a ballpoint pen; theirs must be a tortoiseshell fountain pen they purchased at a flea market and then soaked in solvent overnight to restore its flow. Only Italian or French toothpaste will do. They will never buy soap at the supermarket or eat American cheese or American chocolate. They'll wear something a little old and frayed so long as it was once of superior quality rather than a brand-new article from a low-end chain store. Dandies have their own brand of elitism. From a distance you may think you're looking at the Duke and Duchess of Windsor. Close up you see an aristocrat on a shoestring budget.

When it comes to work, Dandy Bohemians are likely to have a job with at least some relationship to their own artistic pursuits. They loathe working hours as much as the next Bohemian, so positions as editor at large, curator at large, contributing editor or contributing curator have a great deal of appeal. They may write poetry, dance, theater, film, book or art reviews or essays for periodicals or take photographs—anything that allows them to set their own hours so they can eat, drink and create when they please. They may edit other people's manuscripts and films, manage an underground cinema, teach or manage an antiques store with hours by appointment only. As a last resort, they may give guided walking tours. These will always begin at twilight and finish at a pub or at a wine or Champagne bar. They expect you to pick up the tab.

BOHEMIAN NAMES

Bohemians name things: songs, paintings, poems, characters in novels and plays, movements and manifestos. They name their offspring with the same whimsical sensibility with which they name their pets. A Bohemian may use something long and grand: Sebastian, a saintly name that has a cavalier, sophisticated ring, or go political and poetic—Lysistrata. They love names inspired by gods, goddesses, legendary Native Americans such as Hiawatha,[4] bodies of water, rivers,[5] mountains, flowers, fruits and seasons, and they always fall for something mythic and otherworldly—Cosmos, Celeste, Europa, Ganymede, Juno, Io—as if this earth were just one point on their offspring's galactic trip. Fairy Folk Bohemians love all the moons of Uranus, especially Oberon and Titania, named

---

4. Afro-British composer Samuel Coleridge Taylor chose this name for his daughter.

5. Beat poet Gregory Corso and Kay MacDonough named their son Nile.

after characters in Shakespeare's *A Midsummer-Night's Dream.* Puck, Quince and Moth are also contenders, as are names from *Le Morte d'Arthur* by Sir Thomas Malory. Hindu and Sanskrit names are always popular among Zen Bohemians and cosmically inclined world travelers: Chandra, Lakshmi,[6] Shakti, Kali, Rama, Vishnu, to name a few.

Bohemians spurn the mundane and ordinary but may give their children outdated, old-fashioned names with an honesty devoid of artifice: Molly, Luke or Fanny, for instance. A favorite band or singer may also inspire a name: Fleetwood, Jethro, Donovan.

There are those who will name their child in the spirit of wanderlust—nineteenth-century painter Augustus John named one of his children Romilly. Some choose a name from the location of procreation. Thus Paris, Luxor or Marrakech and no doubt Berkeley fall in there someplace.

Bohemians also name themselves, though technically this is renaming. They see themselves as works of art, a dramatic opus, and choose names accordingly. This usually happens after a creative awakening, possibly stirred by excess stimulation: caffeine, conversation, opiates, an art experience or epiphany such as starring in an Andy Warhol film, head trips and road trips. If the awakening is of a spiritual nature the name might be Hindu or Sanskrit, as mentioned above. Bohemians prefer extremes, informal or grandiose. Bohemians may identify with a character in an obscure book or with a historical figure, feeling this name has more resonance, mystery or power and more accurately describes them than the mundane one on their birth certificate.

6.   Poet Ira Cohen, after an admitted "element of slight squareness" in naming his first two children, used "the more academic spelling" of an Indian goddess for his fourth child. His third was Raphael Aladdin.

Bohemians tend to abbreviate, use diminutives, nicknames (White Grape, Cigarette, Moonlight, Fried Eggs, Ultra Violet, Kiki) or a single name.[7] They will also use initials to obscure gender and lowercase initials in defiance of grammatical and societal rules.

Hokusai, a Japanese printmaker in the eighteenth and nineteenth centuries, used nearly a hundred different names. He sometimes signed himself Old Man Mad About Painting.

A Bohemian may also stick with a middle initial that is enigmatically and mysteriously buttressed between the other names. Alice B. Toklas never dropped her *B*. It stood for Babette.

7.   The eighteenth-century French writer and philosopher Voltaire came up with his own name and tossed away François-Marie Arouet.

BOHEMIAN NAME CHANGES

VOLTAIRE	*François-Marie Arouet*
JACK KEROUAC	*Jean-Louis Lebris de Kérouac*
PHARAOH SANDERS	*Farrell Sanders*
DIZZY GILLESPIE	*John Birks Gillespie*
CAB CALLOWAY	*Cabell Calloway III*
BILLIE HOLIDAY	*Eleanora Fagan*
CHET BAKER	*Chesney Henry Baker Jr.*
MAN RAY	*Emmanuel Radnitsky*
MINA LOY	*Mina Gertrude Lowy*
KIKI DE MONTPARNASSE	*Alice Ernestine Prin*
ULTRA VIOLET	*Isabelle Collin Dufresne*
DORA MAAR	*Henriette Theodora Markovitch*
BJÖRK	*Björk Gudmundsdottir*
PABLO PICASSO	*Pablo Diego José Francisco de Paula Juan Nepomuceno Maria de los Remedios Cipriano Santísima Trinidad Ruiz y Picasso*
CAT STEVENS	*Steven Demetre Georgiou*
NICO	*Christa Päffgen*
MAMA CASS ELLIOT	*Ellen Naomi Cohen*
O. HENRY	*William Sydney Porter*
BOB DYLAN	*Robert Allen Zimmerman*
GUILLAUME APOLLINAIRE	*Guillaume Albert Wladimir Alexandre Apollinaire de Kostrowitzky*
H.D.	*Hilda Doolittle*
E. M. FORSTER	*Edward Morgan Forster*
W. H. AUDEN	*Wystan Hugh Auden*
BALTHUS	*Count Balthazar Klossowski de Rola*
GEORGE SAND	*Amandine-Aurore-Lucie Dupin, baronne Dudevant*
CHE GUEVARA	*Ernesto Guevara Lynch de la Serna*

BOHEMIAN BEAUTY, HEALTH AND HYGIENE

Fragrances of the Bohemian

It's a short list, starting with patchouli oil. Overwhelming (like a true Bohemian), it can be worn stylishly by all sexes and also scents the dog, ferret, pygmy hedgehog, skunk, etc. It hangs on everything in the Bohemian dwelling (including those velvet curtains) and gives headaches to people the Bohemian does not consider adequately romantic. Dabbed on handkerchiefs it can be a suitable antidote to anxiety produced by strange, i.e., corporate places.

Patchouli also has a nice ring to it and is a contender for the name of the Bohemian's firstborn.

Other Bohemian scents: sandalwood and vetiver from the local apothecary, health food store or head shop, Kiehl's Chinese Flowers oil, Moroccan or Egyptian fragrances, dark amber in color and very viscous and sweet with notes of frankincense or other exotic resins, and Eau d'Élide by Diptyque. Some Bohemians are old-world and

wear long-forgotten scents, like violet, lilac and rose. Lavender also
figures in the Bohemian fragrance wardrobe and is considered part
of the first aid kit as it's used on burns that are not very serious, say
from candle wax, matches or a grease splatter. Dr. Bronner's soap
(see What's on the Shelves), used for showering, is considered part
of the perfuming process. When Bohemians travel they pick up all
kinds of scents, however. Soaps, powders, oils and fragrances from
abroad figure into the picture, and these scents have many charac-
teristics. Bohemians may find fragrances at flea markets. Half-
empty flacons of Evening in Paris, Septième Sens, Chanel
Gardenia, Niki de St. Phalle, My Sin, anything with an attractive
bottle and a provocative scent. If there were a perfume called Les
Fleurs du Mal, it would have a cult following among Bohemians of
every category, except perhaps for the Zen who is faithful to Dr.
Bronner's. Bohemians often buy soap at the health food store and
may have ayurvedic soap in the bathroom, which they may also use
to wash clothes and pets.

Decorating the Flesh

Bohemians may startle you with their beauty. Frida Kahlo with her
brows unplucked. Her moustache unwaxed, a fuzzy icing topping
her bright red lips.

Kiki de Montparnasse painted her lips like a Cupid's bow and
wore eyeliner drawn out dramatically or painted triangles in multi-
colors on her lids. (She carried her makeup kit everywhere.)

Bohemians may blot out their mouth with nude coverage to
appear all eyes, like chanteuse Françoise Hardy. They might go in
for false eyelashes, like Edie Sedgwick, or let eyeliner smear à la
Nico and Keith Richards.

They may go in for a tattooed face like Vali, known as the witch of Positano. They may henna their hands and feet, dab on a *bindi* or pierce tongue or nose. They may paint and dust themselves with white, like Annie Lennox, or go boyish with no makeup at all, like George Sand.

Bohemians may show up in clown or mime makeup even if they are not coming from a job as a clown or mime. You can blame Picasso for that. It is safe to say that Bohemians love looking strange and aloof. They allow makeup to emphasize not only the features but displays of emotion. This means things can get messy. Black eyeliner drawn out to a fine point, on both the upper and lower lids— with Cleopatra and Nefertiti as their guide—is destined to be ruined, smudged: Maria Callas after a good cry.

Mascara is never tear proof. Bohemians expect to wake up with dark blots around the eyes; besides, it goes with tumbled hair. In fact, Bohemians may go out intentionally with smeary eyes, simply touching up the look they achieved by sleeping it off. Many Bohemians think makeup looks better the next day. Bohemians never use eye-makeup remover. That's what showers are for. You would think Bohemians would go in for black pillowcases for this very reason, but Bohemians are never concerned about evidence left on bed linens.

Men in makeup? A beauty mark on a Dandy of any sex is a thing of beauty. When eye kohl is passed around at a dinner party, ordinary-looking men suddenly gain mystery, soulfulness, an exotic air. Of course the poet and the Beat photographer had this all along; we are speaking of the banker who lives abroad and studies Chinese calligraphy and is only marginally interesting without makeup.

The mouth that whispers the poetry of the soul may be left nude or roughed over with cover stick, but most likely it will be red. Blue red, bright red, orange red, violet red, burnt red with a touch of Pompeii sienna, any red.

This will start out uniformly, following the lip contour or arched like Kiki's, and will be touched up incessantly, at the dinner table, on the sofa, on the street using any polished surface as a mirror. Bohemians like a trademark mouth. Lips might not go on too neatly as the night wears on, due to lighting conditions.

Bohemian lip color will also fade and smear from kisses and be purpled by red wine. The color lingers on the Gitane butts stubbed out on the floor, any floor, and on the wine tumblers, hers and yours. Bohemians do not favor long-wear, kiss-proof red: Bohemian lips are designed to leave traces.

Bohemians don't go in for pastels.

Bohemians find hauntingly lovely shade names and hues at secondhand stores and flea markets, slicker lipsticks from the sixties, and matte theater makeup. They find racy hues at dime stores and, because they are cheap, never feel bad about losing those lipsticks or using them to jot down a phone number. Bohemians like spit-and-dip mascara, but they'll use anything, from Maybelline to M•A•C to Chanel, unless of course they are Zen Bohemians and read all the ingredients. Bohemians are inventive when it comes to makeup. Kiki wet a burned match for her eyebrows. Ever resourceful, Bohemians have also been known to paint with a wet red jelly bean, which dampens nicely as lipstick or rouge, though they don't go in much for rouge unless it comes corked in a bottle or a clay pot from Morocco.

Bohemians finish off with pale powder, brushed on from a box or tin. Bohemians never use bronzer or self-tanner. No sparkles, either, unless it's New Year's Eve and they have gotten ahold of some old gold makeup or dipped into framing or art supplies and dug out the metallic leaf. Bohemians are experts at cultivating the look of being consumptive. Sunlessness. Skin blanched of pigment. Eyes darkened, expanded with belladonna.

Romantic Bohemians of the 1830s used to imbibe a fashionable poison to emulate the poetic, ghostly pallor of Byron and the ethereal complexion of their prima ballerina idol, Maria Taglioni. Bohemians have always been for pale and ghostly skin that's not at all robust, but medieval, doomed, saintlike. Envision the greenish-bluish hue shining through the flesh color in a painting of Christ by Cimabue.

When it comes to nail polish, Bohemians either shun it completely or go all out. Red, violet, green, blue. Sometimes black, silver or gold. Bohemians do things with their hands. Knit, cook, type, talk, dip into photo chemicals and wet clay and rinse paintbrushes in turpentine. Therefore bites and chips are to be expected. All polish is self-administered.

Bohemians may practice extreme beauty. Aboriginal paints, primal streaks, gold leaf or marking pens. Lip liner left off the lips will draw a line to snake around the arm if there's not already a tattoo there.

Gypsy Bohemians may decorate their faces with flower and butterfly motifs and are amenable to a little fairy dust. Zen Bohemians are concerned with perfecting inner and outer harmony. Bare skin and lip balm in a tube or pot might just do it, unless of course they attend one of those dinner parties where the eye kohl is passed around. Rice powder, as opposed to talc, is favored by Zen Bohemians. Bohemians use baby powder in a pinch.

Hair and Grooming

"Make no mistake, if you cut your hair or your moustache, you cut off part of your talent. This external concession, made to the bourgeois feeling of the time, is repeated in your art, and you will soon remove from your imaginative style what you take from your imaginative dress."

—*La Presse*, **22 April 1844**

Even Bohemians have bad hair days. (These, of course, are a different kind of bad.) After three or four glasses of wine they start cutting their bangs, trimming sideburns or cleaning up the goatee with a straight razor. Bohemians may also shave their head or shave patterns in an already short cut. This usually takes a lot more than wine. A Bohemian might, after a few hits on the bong, experiment with facial hair and shave a part in the middle of a moustache, for instance. When this ends up looking ridiculous they will heave a sigh, leave it, then twirl up the ends with wax. This is usually around the time that a third, fourth or fifth earring seems like a good idea.

Sometimes Bohemians let other people cut or groom their hair: friends, lovers, seven-dollar barbers and students in beauty school.

For the most part, Bohemians are not interested in taming their hair. They aspire to rich, dense, savage hair that can be tossed dramatically, twined, woven, braided or flung up, twisted and secured with chopsticks, pencils or paintbrushes. Bohemians of all sexes may have bangs; these will be worn childishly blunt, weirdly short like a medieval cleric, or way too long, the kind of long that prompts family members to say, "You'll go blind like that."

Bohemians, in fact, share all hairstyles from shaven heads to pony-
tails to braided pigtails.

Bohemians have always used hair to protest the status quo.
Shaven foreheads,[8] unshaven facial hair,[9] you name it.

Bohemians are notorious for letting considerable time pass
between shampoos, but that doesn't mean they are not vain.

Bohemians will put flowers, ribbons and trinkets in their hair
or wrap their hair in rags. They groom their hair with scents from
the Orient, pomades that smell of patchouli, neem leaves and rose
water. They will buy hennas from Morocco, but they hardly ever
lighten their hair and never, never do highlights. Bohemians have no
interest in looking like a cheerleader or the Breck girl.

Bohemians cut off all their hair when depressed romantically
or artistically and during any sort of emotional turmoil.[10]

Bohemian females might do a little tweezing under brows or
over a lip, but they don't go in for salon waxes. They consider this
a waste of time that might otherwise be spent sleeping, writing
poetry or making earrings. A unibrow is a feminist proclamation,
and a moustache makes them feel kinship with Frida Kahlo.

8.   In the 1830s, way before the mullet, young men looked to Victor Hugo and
Lord Byron as romantic role models and formed La Société des Latifronts or The
Association of the Noble Brows. According to Gautier, they aspired to "a meas-
ureless brow, the brow of a genius, just like the great men of the time" and "shaved
off an inch or two of hair" at the forehead. Some also shaved all the hair off their
temples. The rest of the hair was long and flowing.

9.   Augustus John kept his beard while in the Canadian army, making him the
only officer serving in the Allied Forces to be allowed to do so—apart, of course,
from King George V. John was also allowed to paint. This didn't last long, however,
as he was sent home after two months following a brawl.

10. Frida Kahlo cut off all her hair in self-destructive lamentation over Diego
Rivera's infidelity.

Shaving legs is for special occasions, like posing for nude photographs or for a sister's wedding, but only if she insists. A Bohemian is more likely to get a buzz cut than shave or home-wax her armpits.

Bohemian guys think the American film director John Waters has a pretty cool moustache since it looks as though it was drawn on with a thin charcoal pencil by a skillful elf, but it's ultimately a little too creepy. But after many glasses of wine . . . well, you never know.

A beard for a Bohemian will range from a few days of shadow —emblematic of intense, tortured thinking and cerebral work around the canvas, typewriter or theater—to a full-blown beard.

Tampering with hair is a cost-effective and powerful way to make striking changes in appearance.

BOHEMIANS LIKE HAIR BY:

JOAN BAEZ	*straight, parted in the middle*
JONI MITCHELL	*straight with bangs*
MARC BOLAN	*curls*
NICO, LOUISE BROOKS & FOUJITA	*bangs*
LORD BYRON	*romantic tumbles*
SINÉAD O'CONNOR	*baldness*
TOM WAITS	*soul patch*
FRIDA KAHLO	*braids, floral hair ornaments, moustache, eyebrows*
PAUL GAUGUIN	*goatee*
NICK CAVE	*sideburns*
SALVADOR DALÍ	*moustache, which he called his antenna to the muses*
ELVIS COSTELLO, VINCENT VAN GOGH & SIGMUND FREUD	*beard*
FRANCESCO CLEMENTE	*crew cut*
KIKI	*pubic hair. (When the artist Foujita commented that Kiki had no pubic hair, she picked up a black crayon and scribbled some on.)*

To name a few.

Hygiene

Bohemians have little regard for a product's intended use. When the Dr. Bronner's liquid soap has been used up to wash the dishes, or when they are at your place, they may wash their hair with Ivory soap. They may use Vaseline to groom, and any cream or lotion of any sort found in the bathroom may be used to moisturize face and body. Olive oil is used in the bath and for massages. Bohemians have been known to save their fingernail clippings in a 35mm film canister and naval fluff in an antique glass jar. Naval fluff is an ideal material for stuffing a small red velvet heart.

BATHING WHEN THERE IS NO HOT WATER

Warm up some water in a pan.
Add a sprig of rosemary, crushed sage or a splash of rose water.
Orange water will do as well.
Rinse underarms or as needed.

BOHEMIAN THREADS

DEFINING COUNTERCULTURE STYLE

The Bohemian expresses eccentricities, poetic anarchy, decadence, newfangledness, revolution, creativity and deviance with personal style. Bohemians devise their own criteria about what is acceptable for the occasion, which will most likely be inappropriate for the occasion, unless, of course, the occasion is strictly Bohemian. When the setting is strictly Bohemian—a cold-reading series at a theater, an absinthe party, a band in a nightclub—anything can happen.

Bohemian fashion is always counterculture but may be adopted, over time, by mainstream society.

Take Jackson Pollock; his bad-boy artist attire was rebellious, part cowboy, part thug. Now his taut but casual look could inspire a jeans ad.

The Primitifs, a group of late eighteenth-century artists, ran around Paris in togas and Phrygian robes, outfits they'd seen on ancient Greek vases. Naturally, Empire waists and classical Greek styles became all the rage a few years later.

Macaw rescued from animal shelter ....

Lace trim cut from vintage slip found at flea market

Lace glove from Dumpster, found in a shoebox of single gloves and handkerchiefs

Vintage underwear with added-on beads worn over bra from the Monoprix in Grasse, France.........

Assorted bangle bracelets .

Antique piano shawl plucked from grandmother's cedar chest ....

Floral skirt picked up in an open-air market in Paracho en route to butterfly migration

Vintage platforms from the Salvation Army

BOHEMIAN DRESSED for INTERVIEW at RECORD STORE

Stingy brim from the 99¢ Store, spray-painted pink

Feather picked up in a state park in northern California

Homemade tie-dyed T-shirt

Hand-woven backpack basket from brother's handbag factory back home in the Philippines

Vintage Sears Wash 'N Wear suit from "clothing-by-the-pound" thrift store

Square brass ring made of handbag fitting / strap attachment

Umbrella picked up at downtown restaurant when left by tourists

Brass chain for vintage Austrian lighter

White bucks refreshed by white paint

BOHEMIAN DRESSED for WEDDING in WOODSTOCK, NY

Bohemian clothing may be anachronistic, distressed, paint streaked, serendipitous, inappropriate for the gender, smocked, embroidered, frayed, fringed, trimmed, shrunken, mismatched, vintage, militaristic, borrowed, custom-made, altered, theatrical, ethnic, folksy, wrinkled, unwashed or new, but it will always be strangely stylish. There is no limit to Bohemian ingenuity. Clothing may be dyed, sleeves and collars may be removed or added, coat linings may be worn as outerwear with a few alterations. Patches, appliqués and fringe may get tacked on, out-of-style accessories may be revived—anything can happen.

Sometimes irreverence is the operative word: Edvard Munch grabbed a pair of scissors and cut off the tails of his evening coat on a whim.

Alfred Jarry went to the opera in Paris in an outfit made of art supplies: white canvas suit and paper shirt, upon which he painted a tie in India ink.

Kiki de Montparnasse, the famous Parisian Bohemian muse, once cut two Schiaparelli dresses in half lengthwise and sewed the mismatched pieces together. She is also known to have pinned a bit of red dress fabric at the collar of a coat and gone naked underneath. Bohemians are famous, notorious even, for shedding clothing for artistic or mirthful reasons.

Fashion designers often troll the Bohemian underworld to glean original ideas, then interpret and sanitize Bohemian innovation for the catwalk.

It's always difficult to say what's in the Bohemian closet. There could be ball gowns, opera coats, velvet capes and smoking jackets hanging next to peacoats, paisley or calico frocks and jeans.

Nouveau Threads

Fashion? The Nouveau Bohemian may be a great stylist and haunt flea markets and forage in the wardrobes of long-deceased relatives. Fashion for the Nouveau is often a blend of new, peppered with vintage and even custom-made clothing (a nineteenth-century practice). The Nouveau will seek out designers who have lived or soaked up the Bohemian life in New York, Paris, Italy, Berlin, Amsterdam or Antwerp.

Nouveaus may adopt any of the Bohemian styles: paint-streaked jeans and ragamuffin shirts or outfits that make you think of girls—or boys—drinking Pernod in Paris during the war; lush outfits worn by counts or countesses—a Nouveau may, in fact, be a count or countess; or clothing native to the country where they happen to buy or rent a villa.

Gypsy Threads

The Gypsy Bohemian is globally conscious when it comes to fashion. It's a global free-for-all, folksy sort of thing. We're referring to authentic national folk costumes and native dress—Indian paisleys, Chinese slippers, floral babushkas from Poland, dashikis, Scottish sporrans, Mexican embroideries, Tyrolean horn buttons, kufi hats, Nehru jackets, Native American beads and turquoise, with maybe a fez thrown in for good measure. The Gypsy Bohemian favors fashion that is unacceptable for conservative business environments: flowing poet shirts, gauzy peasant tops, kaftans, djellabahs, ruffles on shirts and petticoats, gypsy skirts, dirndls, suede vests, embroidered shawls, fringed shawls, velvet capes, ponchos, plumed cavalier hats, floppy felt hats, all kinds of hats, you get the picture.

Languid kimonos hang on doors; the really shredded ones are assigned to decoration exclusively.

Augustus John sported a gypsy hat, silk scarf and gold earring that would become not only his trademark, but required dress for any would-be Bohemian of his time, and that still works now, for that matter.

Poet shirts and ruffled shirts—the Gypsy shares a passion for these items with the Dandy—will be worn with old-man trousers in black gabardine, or possibly jeans. To go to a cocktail party the

Gypsy might toss on a black clerical robe or cassock, à la Rasputin. This doubles as a coffee shop outfit and painter's smock. A straw hat or bandanna will also be worn with this garb in a sunny clime.

Gypsy Bohemians with Fairy leanings choose only the most fluid and elfin elements of the above-mentioned clothing. For this offshoot, it's fairy queen or king meets Arthurian legend meets Pre-Raphaelite. Fairy women tend to model themselves after visions of Guenevere, Titania or Sir John Everett Millais' painting of Ophelia. They favor diaphanous nymphet dresses, skirts, blouses and capes, velvets of all kinds, Empire waists, dryad-worthy prints, florals and leaves. Hair is worn long and wispy, sometimes braided in peculiar configurations, often threaded with ribbons.

Arthurian men do not wear tights, and jeans, in fact, may be the trousers of choice.

Footwear includes Birkenstocks (even models wear them these days, but Bohemians remain steadfast in their appreciation), water buffalo sandals, espadrilles, leather ballet slippers of all hues, slippers from Chinatown in satin brocade, straw or plastic, moccasins, moccasin boots, tall black or brown leather boots regardless of season, clogs and Dr. Scholl's. The Gypsy Bohemian can't resist wooden footwear and flip-flops from bins in supermarkets and drugstores. Gypsy Bohemians wear vintage Earth shoes, but all Gypsy Bohemians prefer to go barefoot.

The Gypsy Bohemian is expert at picking from naked feet splinters and glass acquired from unsanded wooden floors or stepping on shards of broken wineglasses.

Gypsy Bohemian clothing may be noisy and may whistle, rustle, jingle, jangle, tinkle, clink and clang.

Beat Threads

Gritty, severe, casual, maritime, practical, working-class, minimal, sometimes ooh-la-la. Beats look cooler than any other Bohemian. They are the toughest, most tautly attired of all the Bohemians. Indigo, white, putty and black are the main colors, black being the most dominant. Black jeans, black jackets, black wingtips, black sneakers, black ballet slippers, black berets, black sweaters, black shirts, black coffee.

It should be noted that the intellect, the interior life, ideas, poetry, spirituality are more important to the Beat Bohemian than anything exterior.

Outerwear is generally the same for Beats of all sexes and will include a trench coat in black, navy or beige, a camel's-hair coat from a thrift shop or a navy blue peacoat. A corduroy jacket may appear from time to time in the academic as well as the non-academic Beat wardrobe. This will be brown, forest green or burgundy.

The Beat hat collection ranges from fedoras to Greek fisherman's caps. (See Headgear.)

THE BEAT BOHEMIAN GUY

Even the most masculine of the Beats has been known to spruce up his wardrobe with a paisley shirt or Nehru jacket. Life is not just about predictable turtlenecks, jeans, baggy pants that are cuffed and a little too short or too long and sleeveless ribbed undershirts or "wife beaters" so worn, so washed as to be nearly sheer, like diaphanous gauze.

A well-fitting plain white T-shirt with jeans, worn with a belt, is about as Beat as it gets. Role models: Neal Cassady, Jackson

Pollock. Beats also wear T-shirts in black or grey. These will be somewhat snug but never so shrunken as to show the navel.

The Beat may personalize his undershirts by slicing them or burning cigarette holes in them in some sort of pattern. The first cigarette hole is always an accident.

There will be striped sailor shirts borrowed from Picasso's era, turtlenecks in cotton and wool, work shirts in denim or chambray and denim jackets. Plaid also insinuates itself into the Beat Bohemian closet (which may be a suitcase). Beats may wear mismatched plaids. Mexican shirts or any other shirt with the casual, boyish, roughhouse style of Jack Kerouac are Beat favorites. These are generally worn with trousers or jeans, which will be Levi's.

Since cuffs and collars on tailored shirts (white preferred) fray, they are the first things to be cut off for summer apparel. If the Beat Bohemian had a polo shirt, which is not likely, the sleeves and possibly the collar will definitely go, even if the shirt is new. This is antiestablishment protocol and proves he is not a preppy. When a sweatshirt is sliced and diced accordingly, this indicates that he is not a jock. Sweat pants are not worn on any occasion.

DRESSING UP

Suits will most likely be vintage and may be worn with anything from a turtleneck to a shirt missing its sleeves. A simple V-neck vest or undershirt may also underscore the suit, but never a tailored shirt and tie unless the occasion is very, very serious or the Beat is William Burroughs.

Footwear worn with a suit may be dark oxfords and loafers (no metal ornaments or logos), dark work boots (never sandy yellow), flip-flops or leather sandals. A Beat Bohemian would rather be killed in a car accident than wear Tevas.

The dressiest Beat look dips a toe into Dandyism, à la Harlem in the fifties—zoot suits, white shirts and narrow ties and suits that hang just right (whether baggy or fitted), even though they came from a thrift shop, and a great hat. Malcolm X wore a suit. Suits give radical thinking authority.

THE BEAT FEMALE

The idealized look is Audrey Hepburn in *Funny Face*. Black turtleneck. Slim black pants. Flat black shoes flexible enough to allow you to jump onto a chair or table and burst into song or prose. Other footwear: loafers; sling backs, flat and high-heeled, always with a thin heel, never chunky; water buffalo sandals; black Converse sneakers; tall black boots; pointy ankle boots with faux fur trim.

Other closet must-haves: black leotards, sleeveless shell tops, olive drab army fatigues (either top or bottoms, never both together), old-fashioned sailor pants (white for summer, navy for winter, hell to unbutton so she'll just unlace the back), jeans in black and indigo, pleated skirts, A-line skirts, fitted cotton dresses or dresses with a fitted waist and full skirt, long, floppy skirts cut on the bias, Indian skirts, boiled wool jackets, gypsy shirts borrowed from a girlfriend or picked up traveling and all sorts of native clothing picked up on the road. Beats also run around in tailored shirts, his or hers, worn out or vaguely buttoned and tied at the waist.

Zen Threads

Bead necklaces and bracelets are often worn by the Zen. These may be prayer beads of semiprecious stones or rudraksha seeds known as the Eyes of Shiva, bodhi seeds (the Buddha was said to have achieved enlightenment while sitting under a bodhi tree), sandal-wood or jewelry they have made themselves. Zens might wear shiny Chinese pajamas on special outings, chopsticks in their hair and hand-knitted skullcaps. And that's about as exciting as it gets. Their clothing is relatively simple. The T-shirt, possibly tie-dyed, or with a "green" logo or slogan, Polarfleece or Polartec anything, Windbreakers, turtlenecks, bulky sweaters from South America, sweaters knitted by a friend, jeans—their no-frills Beat connection—white cotton drawstring pants, tai-chi outfits, wet suits, snowsuits, overalls, thermal underwear as underwear and outer-wear, down coats (never leather), Alpaca blankets and ponchos in wool or rubber-coated canvas. They will own one pair of Japanese wooden clogs or geta. They intended to wear these when they pur-chased them, but zori, flip-flops, slippers from Chinatown, Pumas or hiking boots always take precedence. Unlike the Beat, the Zen is happy to own a pair of Teva sandals.

Dandy Threads

Dandy Bohemian threads are sprinkled with the classic outré glamour of the smoky Left Bank of the early 1900s, the festive frivolity of the Moulin Rouge. But other looks work just as nicely. *Fin-de-siècle* Vienna. Edwardian pomp. Art Deco decadence. Harlem in its jazzy heyday. And sometimes a Dandy goes over the top into the land of self-made style. These are the fancified, foppish, highly stylized Bohemians who cannot resist smoking jackets (they will have a wardrobe of them, and in candlelight you will not notice the shreds), starched cuffs, ruffled cuffs, ruffled shirts, waistcoats, jackets and knickers of tweed (casual clothing for driving the roadster to the farm in the Catskills and for walks along the moors in Scotland), striped silks, silk monogrammed pajamas bearing initials not their own, Turkish slippers, velvet jackets of burgundy and midnight blue, cigarette holders, pocket watches, walking sticks, monocles, ascots, cuff links, scarves, spats and the occasional fez and velvet eye patch. This is not merely eccentric, but do-it-yourself aristocracy.

A great deal of time and attention goes into the Dandy's attire. Charles Baudelaire, even when destitute, spent up to two hours primping before he'd venture out. Dandies have a dapper and sometimes transgender style. George Sand was dashingly boyish in a man's suit. Alfred Jarry wore women's blouses for comfort. Modigliani wore his scarf flashily. Dandies may wear clothes that are secondhand and frayed, but they will wear them with distinction.

On the femme side: When this Bohemian wears Chanel, it's vintage. Possibly from the Porte de Vanves flea market in Paris. Fishnet stockings. Seamed stockings. A big brooch. Slinky. Filmy. Low cut. Cleavage of any kind could show—front, back, toes. She is decadently louche. The Dandy woman loves fragile vintage gowns, kaftans, tight slinky sheaths reminiscent of Morticia Addams. Irreverence is always lurking in the subconscious mind of the Dandy when she gets dressed—lace, black crepe, nude crepe, satin, outrageous purples, roses, and gowns the colors of claret, absinthe and curaçao with smoky eye shadow to match. She adores vintage platform shoes of Oriental brocade and cigarette holders in mother-of-pearl.

Josephine Baker, who achieved both Bombshell and Bohemian status, was a true classic. She proved a little nudity never hurts either.

The Dandy may break gender rules. She may go as he, and he may wear a lot of she. Dandies are not drag queens, as David Bowie proved in his glam days, but rather men who preen, men who will travel with a trunk full of ties to the Sahara and wear cuff links and white shirts while typing a novel in Tangier. A Dandy will wear a tuxedo to events that are not black tie or while painting in the studio. A female Dandy may embrace Virginia Woolf's *Orlando* and dress androgynously, wavering between the two sexes. A classic man's foxhunting outfit complete with boots, spurs and crop would not be out of the question, especially if she owns a pet beagle.

A Dandy of any sex might carry a large fan to the opera or to the coffee shop. No occasion is too mundane for flamboyance, even in the age of air conditioning. If a Dandy is not able to acquire a magnificent black fan painted with a crescent moon and bats, like the one they saw in a Whistler exhibit, they will have one painted, or paint one themselves.

The Dandy likes to be anachronistic in attire. In Victor Hugo's time, outrageous costumes, deliberately not in style, were designed to wear to opening nights of plays. Nineteenth-century writer Théophile Gautier caused a scandal when he showed up at Hugo's latest play in an evening ensemble he had had custom-made. (Sea green trousers with black velvet stripes at the seams, grey coat lined in green satin, and a ribbon of mottled silk. His doublet was of a Renaissance cut, laced in back and made of what one critic called "silk of a blinding Chinese vermilion." The color was chosen to rattle the grey-loving bourgeoisie. The Dandy never minds a little attention.)

A twenty-first-century Dandy might fancy Victorian attire and, when items are not found at flea markets, have them custom tailored. Dandies also do a lot of their own sewing and mending. A silk shirt or jacket can be easily transformed by replacing commonplace buttons with something more exotic, say, horn or mother-of-pearl.

A Dandy Bohemian with a Beat streak might wear a sharkskin or seersucker suit to the beach with flip-flops and a mesh stingy brim they've spray-painted pink. They take ownership of their clothing and style it with a peculiar irreverence.

Headgear

The Bohemian is not afraid to wear a hat.[11] The Bohemian may, in fact, have more hats than shoes or dinner plates. These will number anywhere from seven to one hundred, but they won't be just any hats.

Ernest Hemingway and Henry Miller wore them, but baseball caps are not the first choice of headgear for the Bohemian. The Bohemian appreciates the proletarian symbolism of a baseball cap but has no interest in wearing sporting goods or anything modeled by "team players," unless it is worn with absolute irreverence, and there is little chance of that with a baseball cap since it's well documented that certain high-profile Americans wear their caps backwards in an affectation of downtown casualness that says, "hey, I'm just a regular Joe." The backward baseball cap, therefore, is even more offensive than the cap worn as it was intended.[12]

11. The relationship between Bohemians and hats dates back to the 1800s. An Englishman visiting the Left Bank of Paris writes: "Fancy these heads and beards under all sorts of caps—Chinese caps, Mandarin caps, Greek skull-caps, English jockey-caps, Russian or Kuzzilbash caps, Middle-age caps (such as are called, in heraldry, caps of maintenance), Spanish nets and striped worsted nightcaps . . . in this . . . costume, the French art student passes his days . . ." From *The Paris Sketch Book,* 1840, by William Makepeace Thackeray.

12. Exception: baseball hats with slogans that are innocently offensive. Writer Tom Robbins, who asserts that Bohemians do not wear baseball caps, says a Hollywood location scout sent a hat to him that reads ODESSA, TEXAS / CHRISTIAN RAT HOLE. Christian is a family name, and a rat hole is a dry oil well. Robbins wears it to fine restaurants.

A black watch cap, fedora, any stingy brim, a deerstalker, a felt beret (Basque only), porkpie, even a homburg will always come first. This goes for men and women. Sometimes a Bohemian will have a signature look. William Burroughs was rarely seen without a fedora unless traveling in Tangier, where he wore a skullcap.

A word about knit caps. Bohemians of all sexes may knit their own hats. Long underground rides from Brooklyn to Fort Washington or from Wandsworth to Notting Hill are an opportunity to make a cap for a lover. Hand-knit hats—never anything *Cat-in-the-Hat* or jester-like—are appropriate for seeing *La Bohème* at the Metropolitan Opera; *La Bohème,* the musical, being a more modern setting, might call for something traditional, like a fedora.

Appropriating a hat from the opposite gender is commonplace. The porkpie, for example, worn by women in the early 1900s and popularized by jazz musicians in the forties and fifties and more recently by Tom Waits, is an acceptable hat for men to wear to a musical, play, nightclub, audition or job interview. The Bohemian cannot, in fact, think of an occasion that's inappropriate for the porkpie.

Do not expect Bohemians to take their hats off indoors unless they are Dandies.

The Bohemian is more likely to get fashion ideas from crime scene photos than from fashion magazines. To wit: The Bohemian has seen the PRESS card sticking out of hatbands in Weegee photos and thinks it's rather stylish. Toothpicks are also tucked into the hatband as part of the Bohemian dental hygiene program. Veils, peacock feathers and plumes, the larger the better, worn tilting backward, are favorites of actresses, poets and costume designers.

Dancers generally prefer scarves.

Driver's caps, skullcaps, bowlers, top hats, Greek fisherman's caps (put on the Bohemian map by Bob Dylan and back on the map by Thom Yorke), engineer's caps, applejacks, Chairman Mao caps in Communist grey, Cossack hats and World War II leather pilot caps with earflaps may insinuate themselves into the Bohemian wardrobe, along with big floppy Hippie hats. Straw hats may be found at the 99¢ store. The Bohemian buys ten of these at a time and customizes them with spray paint, scissors and assorted hatbands.

It is safe to say the Bohemian will not wear a ten-gallon hat, even when riding a horse. This is partly due to the respect they feel for genuine cowboys, and partly because they feel ridiculous when they wear one, or at least they think they would feel ridiculous. They have never tried one on. John Wayne and Garth Brooks made sure of that. Jack Palance is another story—the Bohemian loves the bad guy in a Western.

Bohemians will always have a hat that goes with the vehicle in which they are traveling. Ivy caps and driver's caps are popular with jalopies, roadsters and bicycles, a classic fedora or stingy brim fedora with pointier vehicles.

The babushka, a favorite of the Gypsy Bohemian, may be worn by all sexes and is favored for cross-country trips in caravans.

Fairy types go for flower garlands, but twigs and pussy willows may also find themselves entwined in hair, along with other evidence that they have been communing with nature.

You never know when a Bohemian will show up in a turban.

III
BOHEMIAN
LIFESTYLE

SMOKE

PASTEL: MASKS AND FACES

The light of our cigarettes
Went and came in the gloom:
It was dark in the little room.

Dark, and then, in the dark,
Sudden, a flash, a glow,
And a hand and a ring I know.

And then, through the dark, a flush
Ruddy and vague, the grace
(A rose!) of her lyric face.

—ARTHUR SYMONS

Arthur Symons has been called the poet of cigarette smoke, of
temporary relationships and of sad good-byes.

The Bohemian is a connoisseur of sensation, so there will be smoke. Smoke is the Bohemian's cosmic scrim. It swirls the atmosphere with a foggy fever, an Olympian, cloudlike fairy-fire haze, the smoke of the underworld, the residue of unwholesome and mind-altering acts, the poetic blanket that softens hard edges. Candles, incense, smudge sticks, fireplaces and wood-burning stoves all figure in, but untipped, unfiltered cigarettes are the primary source: Gauloises, Gitanes, Lucky Strikes, Chesterfield Kings, Camels, American Spirits and clove.

Cigarette preference: Cigarettes may also be of the camel-dung-smelling variety picked up abroad or from a tobacco shop, or flat and Turkish, purchased for the exotic box. Black Sobranies (along with Cubans, the good kind) are for special occasions. Emphysema for the Bohemian has a nostalgic ring—it sounds like the name of a maiden aunt.

Serious Bohemians will roll their own using Zig-Zag papers, blues and whites, Chills or Job (everyday), licorice papers (cold weather and after dinner) and a variety of fillers including Drum handrolling tobacco, Bali Red, Zen Natural and Midnight Special, which the Bohemian first picked up in Harlem on the way to a club. It would not be unusual to see a few cigarette holders[1] in use; these are kept in a brass or mother-of-pearl box. Some Bohemians prefer pipes, especially if pipe smoking was frowned upon when they were growing up. If this habit was inherited it will have come from the black sheep of the family, usually an artist, writer or eccentric academic.

Cigarettes may be stubbed out virtually anywhere, from dinner plates and coffee cups to paint palettes, metal surfaces and floors in the home that also doubles as a studio. Jackson Pollock let

1.   Paul Bowles, Hunter S. Thompson and Picasso's muse Dora Maar were big on the cigarette holder.

ash rain and butts fall from his lips onto his canvases to become embedded in the paint he dripped and poured. Ashtrays are rarely emptied, and stubs are savored as relics—of a lover (the brand or lipstick residue can make a Bohemian nostalgic), of smoky at-home salons or artistic debates and heated conversations that carried on until dawn. Not entirely romantic, Bohemians know that lingering cigarette butts may be smoked in desperation, a fact that we discover by page three in Kerouac's *On the Road.*

Bohemians adore being shrouded in smoke. (The air was always thick around the Bloomsbury set at Virginia Woolf's home.) The Bohemian café and jazz club is in a perpetual fog of cigarette smoke—refer to any club scene in any Bohemian movie worth its salt, for example, *The L-Shaped Room* and *Funny Face.* In addition to the room-obscuring effect of smoke, the illicit aspect of tobacco, compounded with its stimulating effect, made it de rigueur among many Bohemians.

"Smoking," says Joanna Richardson in *The Bohemians,* "was one of the first steps in the Romantic initiation." Smoke, in the 1800s, perfumed letters and was exalted in prose and verse. One young Romantic of the 1830s composed the following:

Smoke, smoke! Let's light a cigarette,
And breathe the scented smoke of the cigar.
Alas, life's passing, there's no stopping it,
It is but smoke!

Smoke, smoke! Let us get drunk on dreams,
And ask tobacco for oblivion!
Like cigarettes, all things are brief
In a useless life.

In the 1940s, the French singer André Claveau paid homage to smoke with what could be the Bohemian theme song, "Fumée." (See Sound.)

In 1921 cigarettes were illegal in fourteen states, and similar bills were pending in more than twenty others, giving smoking a delicious counterculture cachet and alarming respectable society. Bohemian poet Edna St. Vincent Millay was expelled from college for smoking.

Other smokable transformative substances have been favored by all genres of Bohemians, from Baudelaire's crowd in nineteenth-century Paris to Beatniks to the Haight-Ashbury Hippies.

According to *Emperors of Dreams* by Mike Jay, in the 1840s, the French doctor Jacques-Joseph Moreau de Tours tried hashish while studying madness. He got the idea that doctors should experience the stuff to get a glimpse of the world inhabited by their patients. It didn't take long for the Bohemians of the day to catch on, and soon they had their own pothouse, the famous Club des Haschischens. Top customers were Charles Baudelaire, Théophile Gautier and Gérard de Nerval.

The Bohemian is enchanted by the scene in *Alice in Wonderland* in which the caterpillar who smokes a hookah, an Oriental water pipe with one or many "tentacles," becomes a butterfly. But trans-formation and mind expansion—reaching a higher plane—are not the only appeal of passing the pipe. The hookah has had a reputa-tion for instigating a luxurious sense of idleness since it appeared on the Western scene in Orientalist paintings nearly two hundred years ago. (Bohemians have always been suspicious of the bourgeois work ethic.)

So wholeheartedly did Bohemians embrace the idea of lighting up—opium, hashish and marijuana—that there is an expansive underground lingo of smoking.

(It should be noted that as Bohemians have a contrarian nature, they may shun smoking because it is expected of them. The Zen Bohemian in particular may shun this habit. Smoking, therefore, is not a prerequisite to Bohemianism.)

Incense is the other main source of smoke. Bohemians are wildly discriminating when it comes to incense and choose only the classics. These will include frankincense in stick, cone and natural resin form; myrrh; sandalwood and almost anything from India or Tibet.

Only the Gypsy/Psychedelic/Hippie Bohemian goes in for patchouli, jasmine, ylang-ylang, amber, vanilla and lotus, while the Zen Bohemian is drawn to smudge sticks (sage and cedar to purify a room) and New Age scents with names like Ocean, Desert and Rain. Zen Bohemians have also been known to burn thin, fragile sticks of Japanese incense (Plum Blossoms, Cherry Blossoms, etc.) placed upright in a small square tile or an urn or bowl filled with sand. Joss sticks may figure in if the Bohemian lives near Chinatown or is a Buddhist.

There is almost always more than one incense burner, and often a collection: blue-painted Chinese porcelain, soapstone, Indian brass, teakwood trays, censers picked up at a flea market in Venice or a bazaar in Istanbul, an aluminum or brass urn-shaped burner from a Greek or Russian Orthodox gift shop that the Bohemian bought while visiting a relative. Bohemians may also have handmade burners from a pottery class or purchased in a craft shop in Woodstock, New York, or New Hope, Pennsylvania.

Very often there will be a drawer where incense, charcoal discs and scads of matches are kept. Misplaced phone numbers may often be found in this drawer.

The ceiling of a Bohemian dwelling must always be repainted when said Bohemian moves out.

DUST

The lint of heroes, the powder of saints, the remnants of stars, grit of meteors. To the Bohemian, dust is a cosmic confectioners' sugar, softly coating all objects and surfaces in myopic finery. Dust obscures edges and reality, newness and pretense. Dust imbues a room with an aura of unself-conscious enchantment. Dust is egalitarian—all objects are equally blurred.

The Bohemian understands the historic, poetic and melancholy nature of dust. To the Bohemian, dust is powder from the wings of moths, ash of Vesuvius, cremains of Joan of Arc, atomic fallout, debris of bombed Berlin, soot brushed from the boots of blue-eyed, black-lunged pubescent chimneysweeps in nineteenth-century London. Dust is the dander of a raja's tiger, the erosion of stones, Aztec temples, sphinxes and palaces, the wayward atoms once part of Pericles, Napoleon, Casanova and Geronimo, the pulverized manuscripts of Debussy, Goethe, Coleridge and Zola, the crumbs of Marie Antoinette's breakfast, powder from her hair, molecules of Cleopatra's black eye kohl and residue from John Wayne Gacy's clown white. Dust is the desiccated petals of poppies and the once flamboyant orchids that grow along the Amazon, it is the spent smoke of opium pipes, the fur of monkeys, literary particles from the Alexandria library, the dust feathered from the furniture of queens.

Romantic Bohemians take the old-world view of dust and see it as beggar's velvet or house moss.

Dusting is, for the Bohemian, counterproductive, a thief of time. When the poem is read aloud or published in a literary

review, when the painting is finally hung on the wall, when the film is premiered, the dust that collected during creative days and nights is of no consequence. It will not be apparent in the work at all or may, in fact, be a part of the work, if you take Jackson Pollock's example. (See Smoke.)

Bohemians are not interested in repetitive tasks; they seek adventure, art, iconoclastic expression. Dusting is a Sisyphean venture. Why bother?

When company comes, it is often unannounced, and the dust will lie upon dusty wood and dusty silver and the room, and the ideas and music will fracture any notion of housecleaning, even coffee cups and glasses and dinner plates are not cleaned but occasionally rinsed, unless, of course, fish has been served, a rule outlined by Quentin Crisp.

Even in the case of a planned event—salon, reading, dinner, visit by curators, collectors or art dealers—there will be no dusting. That goes for patrons, lovers, even mothers. Bohemians embrace the fecund atmosphere of their dwellings, which mirrors the disorganized, listing, spiraling, unsanitized creative thought process, unhygienic, pure, sprung from the feral, ethereal, undusted unconscious. It is an attack on well-scrubbed society, this dustiness, a rebellion against sterility.

Strangely enough, dusting, which happens on rare occasions when the Bohemian is particularly hungover or creatively blocked, may create a meditative state. The destructive act of polishing, useless and futile, may have a cathartic effect and may, in fact, even stir up ideas, militant, controversial, incendiary or gauzy and loosely woven. Dusting tools include a sock, boxer shorts, an old Indian scarf, a shirtsleeve (while being worn), a scrap of canvas or Kleenex.

LIGHT

Natural light is desirable to Bohemians, particularly artists, but—since they have little exposure to it with the hours they keep—it is not the most reliable source of illumination. Late-in-the-day light, twilight, sunset light, moon- and starlight, street lamps, the neon sign across the street or from the diner or bar below—these are the primary sources of light that filter through the mottled glass of the Bohemian's window, falling faintly across the balcony or fire escape (where Bohemians may be found sleeping in summer).

Artificial light is therefore key. Even squatting Bohemians manage to finagle wiring—to an adjoining building, to something on the street. At the very least there will be candles.

Bohemians do not favor fluorescent or track lighting.

Bohemian lighting is more about mood, romance and drama than utilitarianism, unless the Bohemian in question is an artist or writer, in which case there may be a halogen lamp or floodlight clipped to an easel. Photo lamps may be put up over a sink as a temporary measure and end up staying there, but in general, lamps are artfully placed and shaded to enchant a room and are never so harsh as to reveal the Bohemian's devil-may-care housekeeping. Exception: Beats. They sometimes leave things as they find them when they move in. They may put up a Chinese lantern but leave a ceiling fixture or floor lamp without a shade. They intend to get one, somewhere, someday, before they pick up and move again, but in the meanwhile, the naked bulbs are good for photographing visiting writers on the living room couch after sundown, using the old Leica.

Ever resourceful, Bohemians may find vintage or discarded illuminating signs to provide amusement and light: a light that screams SUNOCO, flickers PARIS or CAFÉ MOMUS (a former window display at a specialty store), blazes BAR-B-QUE or flashes a dancing girl. Never an American beer.

Bohemian ceiling lamps may include Chinese lanterns in paper or silk, faded and shredded; mosque lamps; tin, star-shaped ceiling lights from India punched with holes or star motifs; chandeliers of all kinds, from crystal to Venetian glass to wrought iron, even if the ceilings are too low. Wall sconces both electric and with candles also decorate the Bohemian home.

Table lamps include Himalayan salt crystal lamps, Japanese, Tibetan and other paper lanterns—these may be placed on the floor as the Bohemian may spend time sitting on pillows—Tiffany and Bohemian glass lamps, oil lamps with opalescent or iridescent bases, alabaster and porcelain lamps with silk shades embellished with shells, beads or fringe or made out of lacquered brown paper bags or lasagna noodles. (See Nine Bohemian Case Studies—Cody.) Bohemians also use vintage

Chinese tea tins, ginger jars and decorative gas lamps
in the form of assorted gods, goddesses and allegorical
figurines that have been salvaged, found at
flea markets, thrift shops or auctions and
wired to function as lamps. They often
require odd-shaped lightbulbs.

The Bohemian version of a dimmer
switch is fabric—shawls and scarves thrown
over a shade. This method may also be used to
alter the color of the room to, say, rose or yellow.[2] For
special occasions, Bohemians bring out the colored lightbulbs.
Pink, red, blue, yellow, amber, black. It would not be unusual to
find black-light posters of Jimi Hendrix in the Gypsy/Psychedelic
Bohemian home, as well as a Lava lamp bubbling away in a corner.

Candles are used primarily for atmosphere and chiaroscuro.
Candlelight takes the edge off clutter, mutes the blemish of poverty
—the unupholstered, the unplastered, the peeling, the tarnished,
the unfinished. Candlelight relegates dust and dinge to the shadows, antiques all objects in a golden sepia tone and casts an
oscillating incandescence that romanticizes even the sparest of
dwellings. Candlelight elevates the street-picked, the shabby, the
scavenged to haunting grandeur. Candles are also favored by
Bohemians who do not have electricity.

The preferred candle color is white or off-white, though
virtually any color, even black, will do. Candles may be paraffin or
beeswax, hand dipped or not. Bohemians favor clusters of small
votives as well as the voluminous cylindrical candles, the kind
found on church altars. Bohemians have also been known to buy

2.   Jack Kerouac in *The Dharma Bums* writes: "I'd always put my red bandana over
the little wall lamp and put out the ceiling light to make a nice cool red dim scene
to sit and drink wine and talk in."

candles at the corner bodega—these will be tall, glass-encased votives in assorted colors promising LUCK, LOVE or MONEY or featuring saints with bilingual prayers. Bohemians do not buy ornamental candles. Exception: Hippie Bohemians who are shameless in their displays of "decorative" or "craft" candles, including sand candles, rainbow-colored candles and candles in the shape of dragons, unicorns, dolphins, stars, moons, pyramids, etc.

There may, however, be an actual human skull upon which a candle has been placed. Whether candles burn in Chianti bottles, candlesticks, sconces or chandeliers, drips are never a concern. Bohemians never scrape up cascading wax overflows, stalactite drips, spills and splatters whether the wax has dripped down walls, onto tablecloths, tapestries or furniture, or puddled on the floor. This is, in part, due to the fact that Bohemians have little interest in housekeeping (see Dust), but it's more than that. Bohemians take to heart the expression "to wax poetic." Wax marks the passage of time, is a yardstick of sorts. A wax buildup is testimony to late-night and all-night intellectual and quasi-intellectual conversations and soirées, it's tangible residue of creative, radical and romantic exchanges, it's a part of history, it's evidence, it's poetry.

Scented candles are in a class all their own; they are incense substitutes and light is a by-product. Hippie Bohemians will light just about anything and see the beauty in it—strawberry, patchouli, green apple, cinnamon, vanilla. The Fairy Folk Bohemian prefers earthy scents like moss, oak moss, cedar, *fougère,* and ethereal florals like jasmine, hyacinth and orange blossom. Gardenia is too heavy, tea rose too predictable, musk too vulgar.

The Nouveau can afford to buy Diptyque candles. Favorite scents are Figuier, Opoponax, Feu de Bois, Basilique, Oyedo and Jacinthe.

NUDITY

Modesty has never been part of the Bohemian vocabulary.

Where the bourgeois public sees nakedness as something shameful or something to be lusted after, the Bohemian sees nudity as something to celebrate. (These distinctions are articulated in Sir Kenneth Clark's *The Nude.*)

Although Bohemians love to dress up—they see the beauty of the body unclothed. Nudity as a state is liberating, free of class, inhibition, pretense, rank and fashion. It's an opportunity to return to the earth, to create a Utopia uncorrupted by buttons, buckles, zippers, neckties, bow ties. Nudity is egalitarian, and according to Kahlil Gibran's riff on clothes in *The Prophet,* it's spiritual: "Your clothes conceal much of your beauty, yet they hide not the unbeautiful. And though you seek in garments the freedom of privacy, you may find in them a harness and a chain."

In the sixties, baring the body was baring the soul. Flower children were known to lie naked in fields in a group embrace that formed a lotus or star. This was no orgy; they were getting "spiri-

tually aroused." More soul baring occurred when John Lennon and Yoko Ono posed naked before the world on the cover of their album *Two Virgins.*

You never know when a Bohemian might take it all off in private or otherwise.

Allen Ginsberg stripped while reading *Howl* in Los Angeles and challenged a heckler to do the same. "Stand naked before the people," he said. "The poet always stands naked before the world."

Dean Moriarty peels it all off in the car while in Texas and talks his *On the Road* mates into stripping, too. "Now Sal, now Marylou, I want both of you to do as I'm doing, disemburden yourselves of all that clothes—now what's the sense of clothes?"

The night Prohibition went into effect, Greenwich Village Bohemians went pagan and splashed nude in the fountain at Washington Square Park.

Bohemians are just as comfortable naked in your house as theirs. They are, in fact, even comfortable naked on top of your house. The French poet Arthur Rimbaud stripped naked on a roof and hurled his clothing to the street below.

While bourgeois artists of the nineteenth century painted generic and idealized nudes or nudes cloaked in Greek mythology, or religious grandeur, the Bohemian nudes of that time were realistic and sometimes confrontational.

The human form is one of the greatest inspirations to the Bohemian and need not be idealized or respectable;[3] nudity is, to

3.   Manet's *Olympia,* for example, a portrait of a notorious prostitute, or his *Déjeuner sur l'herbe,* a realistic portrait of a nude woman (his muse, Victorine) gazing boldly at the viewer as she's sitting on the grass with well-dressed gentlemen. Gustave Courbet painted a naturalistic, nonidealized torso with vulva for a wealthy Turk, and Viennese artist Egon Schiele was jailed for his graphic nudes, some with legs spread, others with raised skirts. As for Lucien Freud's nudes: no rose-colored glasses here; they are unsympathetically realistic.

the Bohemian, an element of life, everyday life and lowlife included.

Bohemians view nude modeling as a dignified and fairly stress-free form of work: flexible hours, no résumé or references needed. Nude modeling does not demand speaking, lifting, typing, filing, selling, ringing up or serving. (Bohemians make terrible waiters, though they have been known to succeed at juice bars, espresso bars and regular bars.)

Nude modeling, in fact, is one of the few jobs where you get paid for doing virtually nothing yet are the absolute center of attention. Not to mention the added perk of being an instant muse. It's also a job that travels well. There are art schools all over the world, and knowledge of the native tongue is not essential.

During breaks, the Bohemian likes to lounge about in a kimono, or possibly a sarong, occasionally a kaftan or a sheet while stealing peeks at their likeness. The ultimate Bohemian muse, Kiki, arrived at the artist Foujita's studio wearing only an overcoat and shoes.

Bohemians see themselves on equal footing with their models, disrobing just as freely. It is important to note that though Bohemians view nudity as a natural state, they fully understand its shock value. Performance artists almost always toss in a little nudity.[4]

There is always nudity in the Bohemian household. In the Bohemian bathroom there will be a nude sculpture, either something made by a friend or a Greek or Roman replica. There will be

4.   Karen Finley smeared her naked body with chocolate and honey in some of her early pieces. Later, she moved on to peaches and canned yams. Penny Arcade, a former teenage Warhol superstar, bares her breasts as part of her act, which, obviously, is better accepted in Europe than in the United States. In the sixties, the artist Yayoi Kusama staged happenings around New York City, many of which involved revealing her body. One of her self-assumed titles was "The High Priestess of Nudity."

at least one nude charcoal sketch or painting of a former lover or friend or muse. The nude art may be the Bohemian's own work, the art of a friend, or something found at a flea market, on the street or in a Dumpster.

People visiting Bohemians' homes are often shocked to see naked children gamboling about, walking on stilts, jumping on the futon or swinging in the middle of the living room from a rope or handcrafted swing. Bohemians figure the children will have enough constraints imposed upon them later in life.[5]

Adult Bohemians also hang out nude in their homes—painting, writing, sculpting, whatever—and will, in most cases, answer the door in this state if they answer the door at all. Dean Moriarty answers the door naked on several occasions in *On the Road.* Painter Jean-Michel Basquiat shocked his assistant who was meeting him for the first time by answering the door in his birthday suit.

Bohemians are always skinny-dipping and will make home movies of themselves. A member of the Bloomsbury Group, for example, can be seen in footage entitled *Carrington—Home Movies 1929* frolicking naked in a lake with a giant plastic swan.

Bohemians are not nudists, however, and do not frequent nudist colonies. This is considered far too organized and unspontaneous and strikes them as unnatural, something of a fetish or cult. Besides, rules take the pleasure out of nudity. While Bohemians might frequent nude beaches, they are just as likely to disrobe at any beach.

5.   In *On the Road,* Jack Kerouac uses the expression "child of the rainbow" when he sees a friend's naked child on one of his cross-country jaunts.

ASYLUM

HOME AWAY from HOME

'In *that* direction,' the Cat said, waving its right paw round, 'lives a Hatter: and in *that* direction,' waving the other paw, 'lives a March Hare. Visit either you like: they're both mad.'

'But I don't want to go among mad people,' Alice remarked.

'Oh, you ca'n't help that,' said the Cat: 'we're all mad here. I'm mad. You're mad.'

'How do you know I'm mad?' said Alice.

'You must be,' said the Cat, 'or you wouldn't have come here.'

—LEWIS CARROLL, *Alice's Adventures in Wonderland*

Long before artists' retreats, Bohemians recovered, regrouped, chilled, created and mingled in asylums. Vincent van Gogh, Antonin Artaud, Jack Kerouac, Allen Ginsberg, Woody Guthrie, Edie Sedgwick, William Burroughs, Burroughs' editor Carl Solomon, Edvard Munch, Ernest Hemingway, Paul Verlaine—many frail and volatile Bohemians have spent some time in sanatoriums and managed some networking.

In *On the Road,* Kerouac writes: "The only people for me are the mad ones, the ones who are mad to live, mad to talk, mad to be saved, desirous of everything at the same time, the ones . . . who burn, burn, burn, like fabulous yellow roman candles exploding like spiders across the sky."

To Bohemians, there is no shame in experiencing altered mental states and sometimes even a little glory in it.

Real Bohemians rarely go to artist colonies such as Yaddo,[6] MacDowell, Millay or Hedgebrook; nor do they usually apply for grants—those are for organized go-getters. Bohemians have little interest in filling out forms, getting letters of reference and furnishing tax returns. Bohemians in need of a break will simply up and move to, say, Mexico, New Mexico, Provence, Tahiti, Tangier, Key West, Paris, Berlin or California or move in with friends, acquaintances, anyone with a summer cottage, cabin, villa or extra room and a tolerance and/or appreciation of eccentricities. (See On the Road.) When things get really rocky, that's where mental hospitals come in; no application necessary, no waiting, no rejections, no cooking, no housekeeping.

---

6.   Edgar Allan Poe visited the Trasks, who bequeathed the estate but long before it was a colony; novelist Rick Moody is forgiven his Yaddo fellowship for telling all in his mental hospital memoir, *The Black Veil*.

With the amenities provided by the asylum, Bohemians can be quite productive and the experience can even be cathartic. Vincent van Gogh, who voluntarly took up residence at the mental hospital Saint-Paul-de-Mausole in Saint-Rémy, painted constantly during his year there. His work changed poetically and profoundly; it became more convulsive, swirling and pulsating with the supernatural, hallucinogenic feeling of *Starry Night*.

If not on a locked ward and allowed to traverse the grounds, the Bohemian patient may also engage in unartistic recreational activities such as billiards or volleyball. Since medication, usually of a sedative or tranquilizing nature, is widely available and immensely popular in institutions, the Bohemian who, in the outside world, never quite grasped the idea of shuttling a ball over a net or around a gym may find that he or she is equal in skill to the athlete who has downloaded his Thorazine. Furthermore, patients never castigate others for poor performance. Another advantage to the stay besides pumping up the sense of athletic prowess is inspiration. The young girl in sweeping dresses taken from a theatrical closet telling you that her dead grandmother is under her bed might inspire a short story, watercolor or poem at the very least.

The Bohemian is never shy about sharing any alternative or outlaw experience. This includes asylum stays. They will illustrate treatments, painting doctors and wards and discussing the stay as though it were something of notoriety or great prestige.[7]

---

7.   Munch's breakdown prompted him to check himself into a clinic in Copenhagen, where he explored prose poetry, sketched and painted. Mental hospital subject matter is always of interest to the interred artist. Van Gogh painted the head warden and interiors with hospital beds; Munch painted his doctor and sketched himself getting shock treatment, scrawling across the page: "Professor Jacobson electrifies the famous painter Munch and induces male positive and female negative power in his enfeebled brain."

Allen Ginsberg let himself be declared mad (the brainstorm of his friend Lionel Trilling) to beat a criminal rap. He wasn't counting on a locked ward when he landed at Columbia-Presbyterian Psychiatric Institute, but he capitalized on the ordeal; he made a connection with fellow patient Carl Solomon, William Burroughs' editor, and used his stay as a source of inspiration. Upon release, Ginsberg hooked up with Kerouac to coauthor *Pull My Daisy,* which was published, in part, along with something by Solomon about his "incarceration," in the underground magazine *Neurotica.* The title: "Report from the Asylum—Afterthought of a Shock Patient."

"So I had a choice between going to a jail or going to a bughouse like a nice young middle-class student," Allen Ginsberg recounted in an interview. "So I chose to go to a very polite mental hospital. When I left eight months later, they said, 'You were never psychotic. You were just an average neurotic.'"

A Bohemian finds an atmosphere sprinkled with loopiness—a place where all things are possible in the mind—more comfortable than so-called normal environments. If the hospital is a private one, for example, and has a sprawling landscape famous for azaleas, the Bohemian who is not a patient may visit frequently to bask in nature and mingle with the clients who are uninhibited with their imagination. For Bohemians, a mental hospital is a kind of mental health club, a place where they never feel like an outsider or an outcast. In short, they can be themselves. Best of all, people take an interest in their ideas. In an asylum, the things that label them in the outside world as off-the-wall or mad—like allowing feral or farm animals to roam their rooms and take naps on the futon, or devoting an entire room to spiders or a hat collection—are deemed charming eccentricities.

Asylums are, to the Bohemian, always a good cause. Lou Reed and The Velvet Underground performed at a benefit for the New York Society for Clinical Psychiatry. Asylums are also a provocative work environment. Ken Kesey's *One Flew Over the Cuckoo's Nest* is proof of that.

Bohemianism and so-called madness share an outcast sensibility. In her introduction to *Antonin Artaud, Selected Writings,* Susan Sontag comments: "A mad person is someone whose voice society doesn't want to listen to, whose behavior is intolerable, who ought to be suppressed."

Sanity and madness were favorite topics of Artaud. In and out of hospitals from midadolescence on, he was always grimacing during roles that required composure, creating work that was banned before production. "I am a fanatic, not a madman," he wrote. Artaud was a Bohemian ahead of his time, into peyote, astrology, tarot, *The Tibetan Book of the Dead* and true alternative thinking, deranged thinking.

We would be remiss if we did not mention that freedom-loving Bohemians eventually feel a horrible sense of confinement in institutions. Routine, comforting for a fleeting moment when all has been chaotic, is never welcome for long. That's when, if possible, it's time to check out.[8]

Contemporary Bohemians out on a limb might be inclined to check out those ads for detox and substance abuse research programs that can be found in the back of *The Village Voice* and other alternative press, offering money for a few weeks or months of "study."

8.   Not everyone checks out, though. Some Bohemians find reality a bitter pill. Romantic poet Antoni Deschamps was mad for four years but stayed in an asylum thirty-five years, until he died.

ON THE ROAD

They travel inordinately, incessantly, restlessly; observing, free-loading, freewheeling, free loving, freedom bound, drinking, mountain climbing, smoking what comes their way, taking jobs, taking notes, taking photos, typing away in the room at night, maybe all night. Run-on sentences happen to Bohemians on the road because they can't stop to edit—they just keep on talking or writing. They may never find themselves at a dead end, but there'll be plenty of detours and no regard for speed limits.

Bohemians travel to the following places: Mexico, Morocco, Greece, Prague, San Francisco, New York, Berlin, Paris or anywhere the lodging is free, under the guises of finishing the manuscript, helping you edit or finish your manuscript, detoxing, retoxing or painting. Because they are entertaining and engaging, dazzling any room they enter with the stardust of irreverence, the Bohemian is always welcome. For a while.

Bohemians shun tourist attractions. The Bohemian has been to Paris ten times yet has never been to the Eiffel Tower, and when they do, always by accident, end up at a tourist attraction, they'll get there so late it will be closed. They would prefer to go to dinner in a restaurant in the slums (Belleville or La Goutte d'or) to experience something real. Bohemians distance themselves from American tourists especially.

While on the road, Bohemians will sleep anywhere from hammocks to haystacks, and if you believe Jack Kerouac, on unbearably hot humid nights in rural Mexico, Bohemians will sleep, literally, on the road. Bohemians do not stay in four-star hotels. Bohemian hotels, in fact, don't usually have stars.

Bohemians believe in bartering.

They'll happily paint a picture of the inn or the owner's daughter, sing an aria, play a madrigal, dedicate the book, walk the dog, read your palm, do your cards or put up a deck so they can stay an extra week or month. There's no telling how long the Bohemian will stay.

WHEELS

Bohemians have cool cars. Even if it's a jalopy, it will turn heads as they drive by. This may be because of the artistic embellishment, vintage style or vintage muffler.

Bohemians have two kinds of relationships with their cars: reverent and reckless.

They'll bang out tunes on the dashboard until it's concave, go beyond the speedometer on a cross-country trip; once it breaks, speed becomes intuitive.

On the other hand, they'll talk about their '67 Volvo, constantly telling everyone it's got 300,000 miles on it, it's the greatest car on earth and that they just drove it cross-country and back without incident.

Bohemians make no distinction between poetic license and driver's license. When it comes to driving, they have a communal sensibility. If someone in the car has a license, they feel it applies to anyone at the wheel. Sometimes cops even buy this. Just read *On the Road*.

Bohemians on the road see speed limits as departure points, something to transcend. They'll get the pedal to the metal just to feel the wind rush through their hair and to see how far they can push the vehicle.

Bohemians get pulled over frequently for myriad and obvious reasons.

Driving Rules, or Vehicle Manifesto

1. Bohemians do not usually buy cars made in the country they live in.

2. The vehicle, whenever possible, will be a standard.

3. The vehicle will be preowned. Bohemians recycle old dependable and undependable vehicles, many of which are not great on gas. The main criteria is that they be (a) vintage and (b) cool. Vehicles include: army Jeeps, hearses, school buses, taxi cabs, ambulances, delivery vans, circus caravans, milk trucks.

4. Every road sign is a suggestion. This includes destinations and speed limits.

CHOICE WHEELS

A 1970 Eldorado.

Volvos, obviously.

A prewar Citroën with running board.

A Citroën DS 19 in its original state, never repainted. (A Bohemian appreciates a car driven by French presidents. See *The Day of the Jackal,* 1973 film version.)

Citroën's Chapron le Dandy or the more orthopedic Dyane in an unnamable color between putty and khaki.

A 1969 BMW 2002 series in the original silver (preferred by actors in San Francisco who like to make mercurial entrances and exits).

A Deux Chevaux (2CV).

An Austin Mini.

The original Mini Cooper.

A 1966 Chevrolet Corvair.

A huge 1972 Pontiac Catalina convertible in flat grey, possibly primer, with hole punched in roof that occurred during a highly animated conversation, or so they say.

A two-tone 1965 Galaxie 500 with a light blue body, black hood. It overheats a lot but what do you expect for a hundred bucks.

A peppermint red-and-white Rambler from the late fifties. Smells strangely like a weasel but what do you expect for a hundred bucks.

A Manza convertible.

A 1961 Corvair hardtop in pistachio green.

A Karmann Ghia in a putrid yellow.

A Ford woody station wagon from the forties. The backseat has a nice view of the road due to the hole in the floor.

A 1959 Morris Traveller.

A 1958 Road Rover in cloudy blue.

A pre-1970 VW Beetle or VW bus, possibly early seventies, but never a new one.

If they ride a motorcycle it will be a BSA, Triumph or Norton from the sixties, never a Harley—only Che Guevara could get away with that.[9]

The Bohemian dreams of owning an Airstream (although technically not wheels), the ultimate caravan. It would make an ideal home.

Not only will Bohemians not purchase SUVs, they are embarrassed to accept rides in them, as though their physical presence in the vehicle will contribute directly to global warming, America's presence in the Middle East, etc.

Bohemians also name their vehicles. "Further" was the name of Ken Kesey's Day-Glo-painted school bus, nicknamed the "Prankster bus," and "the gangster getaway car" is what the poet Herbert Gold calls his Citroën in his cultural autobiography *Bohemia*.

9.   Che Guevara and friend toured South America on a Harley Davidson posing as leprologists when crossing borders. Guevara documented their Bohemian lifestyle—brawls and romantic adventures—in *The Motorcycle Diaries*. The trip opened him to greater social consciousness.

CUSTOMIZING THE VEHICLE

The ceiling of nonconvertible cars may feature floppy fabric that has been tacked up, possibly the dark blue of an Egyptian sky with gold stars, paisley or an Indian bedspread.

Towels on driver and passenger seats cover revealed springs and will be changed seasonally or as needed.

Rope to tie the door shut.

Duct tape as needed.

Curtains on vans.

The ceiling/roof of the van or bus may be painted with swirling Day-Glo patterns.

Hand-painted flowers on exterior of van or bus, never airbrushing.

Slogans. These include:

THERE AIN'T NO DEVIL THAT'S GOD WHEN HE'S DRUNK and I'M NOT HERE, THIS ISN'T HAPPENING.

Bohemians may forsake cars altogether and for crosstown commutes ride a bicycle, unicycle, skateboard or scooter. Bohemians do not own Rollerblades and find them more disturbing than the most expensive automobile or a membership in a prestigious health club.

Buses, subways and hitchhiking are other means of Bohemian transport. Jumping into boxcars is no longer viable.

Bohemians in a romantic but solitary mood may buy a train ticket for no reason in particular, drink wine and knit or read or write a short story or begin a song cycle and feel the rush of the landscape. They will also consider moving to their destination. The ticket is always one-way.

STATIONERY,
CALLING CARDS, ETC.

Bohemians do not have business cards, but they'll gladly use yours.

They will write their address and phone number, when they have a phone, on the back of any card—yours or the one from the coffee shop or diner. Usually, however, they will have some scrap of paper or announcement for an art opening, concert, play, reading or performance, and if not, there's always a matchbook or a cigarette box.[10] When all else fails, and if smitten enough, Bohemians will write your contact information on their hand or wrist. A book or film you suggest may end up scribbled on skin, too.

Notes are often written with art supplies. A conté crayon, pastels, charcoal pencil, an HB or a rich, soft 6B pencil. Never a number 2, the one required for filling out little squares or circles on a form or test.

---

10. Modigliani used the back of a Gitane box as a calling card.

Bohemians use pens that tend to leak. They use old Mont Blancs and antique nibs with spready, bleedy vintage inks chosen for the name or bottle or color—deep violets, inks the color of wine, blood or the blue that reminds them of the eight months they spent by the sea. Bohemians often have stained fingers.

Bohemians write with paintbrushes, using watercolor, gouache, tempera, acrylic, even oil paint, whatever is at hand, or they'll type on an old Underwood or the Remington Noiseless from the south of France that drops the *y* because they can't be bothered to have it repaired; besides, it's got character. Bohemian writers have a romantic attachment to their typewriters and are always reluctant to lend them to friends, even for a day. It is unrealistic to assume that all Bohemians have typewriters, however. Some write everything longhand, including invoices. When the recipient contacts the Bohemian to say they cannot accept a handwritten invoice, the Bohemian politely thanks them in advance for typing it for them since they do not have the means, and by this they mean inclination or desire.

Bohemians have also been known to write poetry with gout medicine (Coleridge when out of ink) and messages in blood, though these are not usually happy missives.[11]

Any and every scrap of paper from menu to cocktail napkin to coaster is a surface worthy of the pen. In addition to addresses and impromptu poetry, whimsical drawings and love letters may be scrawled on these papers.

Love letters deserve special attention. These are not printed on stationery (unless Bohemians have their own letterpress) from the chic little printer on the rue de Bac, Dempsey & Carroll, Mrs.

---

11. Norwegian painter Per Krohg wrote on the mirror, "ADIEU, LUCY" with blood from his slashed wrist before ending it all by hanging himself in his Paris studio.

Strong or Tiffany. Bohemians write letters on clamshells. On any scrap of paper, watercolor paper, newsprint, butcher paper, rice paper, joss paper, origami squares, papyrus, pasta boxes, birch bark that has peeled off in large sheets from the tree, pages torn from outdated encyclopedias, pages torn from a turn-of-the-century ledger once belonging to a haberdashery or a time log from a defunct coal mine in Scranton, Pennsylvania, antique prints from the flea market, wallpaper, fabric, paper bags, the receipt from the liquor store. They draw animals or send the nude they drew of the lover and draw the lover from memory on the envelope. They may spill wine on their letters or burn the edges. Much Bohemian correspondence is scented with smoke. Sealing wax is also favored.

Bohemians always assume their correspondence, even if they are destitute and unknown, will turn up in a museum, be auctioned off at Christie's, be reproduced in a book or be useful, if not for their biography, as material that defines an emotion or epoch.

ELIXIRS, ETC.

"One must be drunk always," wrote Charles Baudelaire. "If you would not feel the horrible burden of Time that breaks your shoulders and bows you to the earth, you must intoxicate yourself unceasingly. But with what? With wine, poetry, or with virtue, your choice. But intoxicate yourself."

Much literary and painterly work can be chalked up to intoxicated or altered states and the substances that produce them.

It is difficult to expound upon Bohemian intoxication in strictly liquid terms, and any meditation on elixirs and other substances is bound to take detours and back roads and maybe even do a little astral traveling. Swirls of laudanum fueled the majestic cadence and incandescent Xanadu caverns of Samuel Taylor Coleridge's "Kubla Khan"; green tea is declared the culprit of one of the deliriously paranoid haunted tales of Joseph Sheridan Le Fanu; it was alcohol, including absinthe, that fueled Edgar Allan Poe's heart-throbbed delirium and horror. His friend John R. Thompson, a newspaper editor, wrote that Poe was lost in "dreamy abstraction," always wandering hazily in "the shady realm of ideas"; Thomas De Quincey waxed eloquently about the insufferable splendor (and later the despair) of opiated dreams in *Confessions of an English Opium-Eater;* and laudanum surely had a little sway over the wildly tortured, otherworldly writings of Antonin Artaud and Toulouse-Lautrec and his absinthe-soaked nights at the Moulin Rouge. His demonic, greenish, underlit characters seem to speak to his 160-proof habit.

It goes without saying that Bohemian artists crave altered states and heightened experience, but even that convention may be shunned. It is said that the French author Henry Murger and his friends were water drinkers, abstinent in defiance of all that idle swilling in cafés. There have been other, more recent Bohemian teetotalers, some vowing sobriety because they were appalled by the savage habits of the likes of Hemingway, but most of these are not household names. Infamy and celebrity, alas, often go hand in hand with "bottoms up."

With risk and excess comes the inevitability of unhappy spirals into basements blooming with ghouls, night sweats and no exits. But the Bohemian is always willing to take the risk and journey to the fringe, the heights, the lower depths, to experience an altered state.

Absinthe

Contrary to popular belief, red wine is not the first choice of the serious Bohemian. It's not beer or scotch, either. It is absinthe—potent, dangerous and outlawed, a symbol of inspiration and daring—that best embodies the Bohemian spirit.

Absinthe, distilled from the hallucinogenic herb wormwood, was the drink of Bohemian artists during the late nineteenth century. The preferred method of drinking the bitter, 160-proof elixir was to pour water into it over a latticed spoon holding a sugar cube, causing the brilliant emerald liqueur to turn first milky green and finally opalescent. An absinthe drinker recently back from Prague says that sometimes the sugar is ignited so it caramelizes before it is dipped into the drink. Bohemians have also been known to drink it straight.

Precursor to the hallucinogens extolled by Timothy Leary, absinthe, also known as *la fée verte* (the green fairy), would still be the quintessential Bohemian drink if it were more accessible. It's banned in all but a few countries, even though the nerve-damaging chemical, thujone, has been reduced, rendering it nontoxic unless enormous quantities are consumed. Pernod, the colorless, worm-wood-free anisette cousin, is a poor substitute; all that remains of its predecessor's charm is the anise flavor and the famous distiller's name. Nonetheless, this neo-absinthe, if you will, is still the drink of choice for Bohemians nostalgic for the nocturnal lifestyle of the tipsy artists and writers they revere and emulate. The courage to be avant-garde, literary, painterly and enchanted by fantasy has certainly never been hindered by absinthe. Oscar Wilde, Evelyn Waugh, Toulouse-Lautrec, Somerset Maugham, Hemingway, van Gogh, Gauguin, Degas, Rimbaud, Verlaine, Maurice Barrymore (father to John, Ethel and Lionel), Edgar Allan Poe, Erik Satie, even Picasso, albeit briefly, were consumed by what puritanical reformists called "bottle madness" or "the green curse."

Truth be told, drink does not the Bohemian make; Bohemians can lighten up, loosen up, jangle verses and groove and scat under the influence of any beverage, from strong coffee to room-temperature retsina to a chilled and frothy Negra Modelo, but it is the spirit of absinthe—the irreverence, the potency, the out-and-out severity and its kinship with dream states—that makes it iconic.

Bohemians who have friends traveling to Spain, England, the Czech Republic, Japan, Andorra, Denmark, Portugal, Ibiza and the Netherlands inevitably ask that they bring back some of the taboo liqueur, if only to taste a legend and to see if their creativity burgeons under the influence. They may also order it online.[12]

The Bohemian is not looking to get annihilated or simply intoxicated but is seeking, above all, to ward off complacency with revolutionary splendor. Hemingway, after all, drank absinthe for its "idea-changing" effect.

In *For Whom the Bell Tolls* he writes: "One cup of it took the place of the evening papers, of all the old evenings in cafés, of all the chestnut trees that would be in bloom now in this month, of all the great slow horses of the outer boulevards, of book shops, of kiosks, and of galleries . . . of all the things he had enjoyed and forgotten and that came back to him when he tasted that opaque, bitter, tongue-numbing, brain-warming, stomach-warming, idea-changing liquid alchemy."

Oscar Wilde writes: "After the first glass you see things as you wish they were. After the second, you see things as they are not. Finally you see things as they really are, and that is the most horrible thing in the world." And, on a more positive note: "What difference is there between a glass of absinthe and a sunset?"

As for the recipes for faux absinthe, few Bohemians can be bothered with them. Unless it's a special occasion they prefer to open a bottle of Chianti, a Chilean red or a French table wine.

---

12. If a Bohemian asks to use your credit card to order something online, it will be for antique books, music, Allen Ginsberg on tape, art supplies or absinthe.

TWO ABSINTHE RECIPES

from James Rowe, bartender at Jerry's, New York City

ABSINTHE I

wormwood, a few ounces

3 cinnamon sticks

15 star anise

2 tbs. sugar

1 vanilla bean

1 bottle vodka

Jam all the ingredients into vodka bottle and let steep for one week.

ABSINTHE II, for the lazy

Steep wormwood in bottle of Ricard or Pernod.

Note from James: Absinthe tastes so hideously rank that people started adding other extra ingredients like lavender, cloves, cinnamon, mostly anise, maybe thyme, etc. But you don't want to get too *gourmand;* if you put too many herbs in you're wasting your time because the wormwood is still going to taste nasty.

Wine

The Bohemian's version of happy hour is the art opening: free admission to view art and free alcohol. Even the most devout red-wine drinker has been known to dabble in cheap Chardonnay in a plastic cup at an opening. Bohemians are likely to be more critical of the work than the wine.

Here they can flirt, talk shop, critique, run into friends, maybe even critics and dealers.

Bohemians rarely have deluxe corkscrews, but this does not mean they partake of the screw-cap variety of wine. They pretty much insist upon a cork. They know what *mis en bouteille* means and appreciate the sediment in a vintage Château Margaux, but they are by no means snobs. France, Italy, Chile, Australia—decent wine from any country will do.

Wine is an integral part of everyday life for the Bohemian; left-over wine may be part of lunch or even breakfast, which may be eaten at noon or whenever the internal Bohemian wake-up alarm goes off.

Champagne

Bohemians never turn down Champagne; they are seduced by the reckless cork with its element of risk. Unless they are Nouveau Bohemians, they also never order it. The Champagne of choice is Nicolas Feuillatte. Its owner calls it the Champagne of the "Bourgeois Bohème." Bohemians find this oxymoron infinitely amusing.

Beer

Proletariat Bohemians drink beer, but not just any beer. Their esoteric tastes require noncommercial brands. A microbrewery or beer from a third-world country will do, but they are usually wary of anything mass advertised or with chemically induced foam. They are also disdainful of brands drunk by yuppies, investment bankers and Super Bowl fans. True Bohemian beer, without a doubt, will be preferred, most notably Pilsner Urquel, which is brewed in Pilsen in the part of the Czech Republic known as Bohemia. Hardly newfangled, it still has the hoppy herbal taste of the original recipe.

This doesn't mean that Bohemians will turn down a cold Budweiser on a hot summer night. Bohemians take kindly to complimentary beverages.

Coffee

Bohemians generally start their day, regardless of the hour they wake up, with coffee. This may be espresso, Turkish, French press, percolated, drip (either with a conventional pot or simply the plastic top portion fitted over a mug into which hot water is poured) or boiled—in extreme times it may even be instant—but it is never decaffeinated. As for the kind of coffee, anything not obviously commercial goes, from French roast (southern Bohemians may have theirs with chicory), Peruvian or Sumatran to organic or even El Pico in the vacuum-packed yellow package. Bohemians do not favor complicated coffees or Starbucks. Flavored coffees are not the Bohemian's first choice, but the Bohemian has been known to stoop to a cup of French vanilla or hazelnut rather than go without.

Coffee is one of the most important ingredients, if not the most important beverage, in the Bohemian lifestyle—it has been fueling revolutionary ideas and caffeinating conversations of poetic, orchestral, dramatic, painterly and literary persuasions in the West since the first European coffeehouse opened in Venice. (Caffeine is a drug, after all, and the Bohemian is under its spell.) Not just any cup of joe in any place will do. For centuries, Caffé Florian was the favorite of Bohemians (this includes the privileged Nouveau Bohemians): Byron, Proust, Goethe, Stravinsky and Modigliani. It's hardly Bohemian today, but contemporary Bohemians appreciate its cachet and wouldn't dream of visiting Venice without paying homage.

Slaughter's Coffee-house was the Bohemian hangout in Georgian London. Crowded, loud, raucous and smoky, like most London coffeehouses, its underground atmosphere spawned subversive dialogue, uninhibited speech and controversial, modern ideas.

Meanwhile, in Paris, Le Procope attracted poets (La Fontaine, Verlaine), writers (Balzac, George Sand, Hugo, Diderot, Voltaire, Anatole France), dramatists (Beaumarchais), painters (J. L. David), philosophers (Rousseau) and revolutionaries (Robespierre, Danton, Marat). Even Benjamin Franklin stopped by.

It's rumored that Voltaire drank forty cups of coffee mixed with chocolate every day at the café. (Like the Florian, the Procope is still up and brewing.) At the height of the coffee craze, the medical establishment, appalled by the nerve-jangling effect of coffee, warned the public with the following report: "The sufferer [from coffee addiction] is tremulous and loses his self-command; he is subject to fits of agitation and depression. He loses color and has a haggard appearance. . . . As with other such agents, a renewed dose of the poison gives temporary relief, but at the cost of future misery."

In Vienna, writers took to coffeehouses like Beatniks to bongos. Cafés started stocking writing supplies. Out of coffee? Out of paper? Out of ink? No problem. Some writers even gave the café as their address and received mail there.

Fin-de-siècle Vienna, the cradle of modernism, boasted a staggering number of coffeehouses—around six hundred or so. Of these, the Café Central rose to the top, attracting nobility, students, Bohemians, journalists and merchants. Czech architect Adolph Loos, who wrote that ornament was a crime, became an ornament himself at the Café Central. Commissioned to design a café, he came up with the streamlined, embellishment-free Café Museum adjacent to the House of the Secession. The Café was soon the hangout of Gustav Klimt, Egon Schiele and the rest of the Viennese avant-garde.

The intellectual and creative activity sizzling inside coffeehouses led many political and religious leaders to believe them to be hotbeds of rebellion and decree them illegal.

Apparently, there was something to these fears. At the Procope in Paris, revolutionaries Robespierre, Danton and Marat decided that heads were going to roll. On the other side of the Atlantic, John Adams and Paul Revere chose the Green Dragon coffeehouse in Boston to plot against the British. Lenin and Trotsky met regularly at the Café Central in Vienna in 1917 before kicking off their revolution.

Tea

Some Bohemians, especially Zen Bohemians, start their day with tea.

Tea will be Darjeeling, English, Irish or Scottish Breakfast, or any black tea from China or India, always loose and made in a pot. The Bohemian takes tea brewing seriously and always adds one for the pot.

Lapsang Souchong in the morning is the smoky choice of Beats, as it goes well with a cigarette, but it is also a must for the Bohemian who wears silk paisley shawls and Virginia Woolf hair. It

should be noted that Beats will drink any supermarket black tea from bags, but black coffee is usually the first choice.

If a Dandy drinks tea from a bag, it must be in a linen or silk sachet and preferably scented with bergamot. Nouveau Bohemians who have read J. K. Huysmans' *Against the Grain* are frustrated by their inability to find the "impeccable blends of Si-a-Fayoun, Mo-you-tann and Khansky—yellow teas imported from China into Russia by special caravans." They are planning a special tea trip to China just to find them. They plan to drink them from delicate eggshell china in keeping with Huysmans' novel. In the meantime, they amuse themselves with Blooming Green Peony, "Ching Ming" Lung Ching and oolong from Fenghuang Shuixian.

White teas such as Chinese Silver Needle, Chinese Mutan White or Ceylon Silver Tips (the tea is actually pale pink) are the choice of Zen Bohemians before morning meditation or Wu Ming qigong. A grassy cup of Sencha is also a Zen favorite. Bohemians also appreciate black tea from France—especially from Mariage Frères—and they cannot resist tea from Fortnum & Mason, by appointment to her Royal Majesty. Later they will use the tin for paintbrushes, chopsticks or kitchen utensils.

Bohemians adore buying loose, exotic-sounding tea in bulk from tea shops in London or Scotland—but tea shops in, say, the West Village in New York will do in a pinch. Bohemians do not take milk or cream in their tea, as it goes bad in electricity-free squats, but many are partial to lemon, which does well on a windowsill in most seasons and is considered a source of vitamin C.

Sugar will be in packets taken from a diner or in cubes taken from a restaurant; Bohemians seldom actually buy sugar. They consider buying it an unnecessary extravagance; with packets thrown wastefully into deli to-go bags and voluptuously accessible on restaurant tables, it's part of the Bohemian gratuity system. Cubes are dispensed with Grandmother's sugar tongs, silver and always a bit tarnished. Teacups will be odd sorts bought from flea markets or inherited. The saucers, if there are matching saucers, will only match the teacups as a random act.

Gypsy and Zen Bohemians may drink green tea. The tea of choice is loose Gunpowder or Green Thunder, which is coiled tightly as a fist and unfurls in the pot when hot water is poured over it, until the water is as dense with leaves as the seaweed-swirling Sargasso Sea; it is consumed until all hours when work requires alertness and lucidity.

Bohemians do not drink any beverage that has gone through a decaffeination process.

HERBAL TEAS, OR BOHEMIAN HEALTHCARE

These range from peppermint, chamomile and rose hip to all manner of witchy medicinal herbs procured from those apothecaries and health food stores that buy in bulk and scoop out quantities from large glass jars into small brown paper bags. Here it might be appropriate to say that most Bohemians do not have health insurance. Bohemians refer not to *The American Medical Association Guide to Your Family's Symptoms* but to Edgar Cayce, homeopathy guides and *The Herb Book* by John Lust for their sore throats, migraines and hangovers. Bohemians rarely have need for insomnia treatment, as this is considered a natural and/or desirable state.

COUNTERCULTURE CUISINE

Testicles of lamb with a pinch of cinnamon

Sparrows' brains with chickpea broth sprinkled with clover seeds

Lambs' ears stewed with sorrel

Boar shank with black radishes

Frog pasties

There are many recipes that contradict the traditional Bohemian empathy for wildlife. (See Wildlife.) Bohemian cuisine is not just about red wine, bread and cheese, or red wine, bread and spaghetti or red wine, bread and mussels. Bohemians embrace, whenever possible, unconventional food and eating habits. That doesn't mean they might not eat cheese spread or Spam from the tin, but they appreciate the exotic, antiquated, and elaborate, and no matter how humble the food, they will usually create an atmosphere to go with the meal.

Bohemians like to eat and prepare food from countries not native to them, or from another time period. They might throw a medieval banquet in the woods with homemade mead and quails and capons or other animals roasted on a spit. These will be eaten in true medieval style, without forks. Costumes required. You never know when some Bohemian will bring chopsticks just for kicks. Bohemians also excel at picnics.

Bohemians may also custom design a meal for a guest. Alice B. Toklas created a recipe for cold bass decorated à la Picasso for Picasso. It involved abstract decorations using mayonnaise and red sauce.

Bohemians will create menus that are color based—all white food, for example, or a red, white and blue menu—whatever strikes them at the moment if it's in season and in the budget. They also delight in breaking dietary rules. Alfred Jarry, the notorious poet of the Parisian avant-garde, ate his desserts first and finished with an appetizer. Virginia Woolf and the Bloomsbury set rejected the traditional Victorian table and did away with napkins and came up with a recipe for mouse on toast. Bohemians may also scoff at nutrition and specialize in sweets. In a book describing the lunch of a Dandy Bohemian based on French poet Baudelaire, the character "took his *déjeuner* of citron, preserves and sugar candy."

On any given night, dinner might be Heinz baked beans, Dinty Moore beef stew on toast, or sautéed kidneys with port wine sauce and Saltines or Bath Olivers eaten by candlelight with music by Bob Dylan or Salif Keita if there is electricity; if not, the Bohemian will play a little guitar or banjo or perhaps a flute before eating; otherwise there is always the Victrola. The guests will have to crank it while they cook. The Bohemian may also put on a rather elaborate costume for a themed meal and expect you to dress up, too. China and flatware are generally mismatched.

The music that goes with breakfast will be whatever was on the turntable from last night, unless it's heavy on the drums. (See Sound.) Breakfast may be coffee, and if that's all, the Bohemian will add lots of nondairy creamer or half and half and sugar taken from the diner[13] the day before "to make it go farther" and "as nourishment, as energy."[14] Breakfast is never taken before noon.

When *you're* cooking, Bohemians are easy to please. Hamburgers, cheeseburgers, Wiener schnitzel, pirogues, matzo ball soup, fried eels, macaroni and cheese, meat loaf, they eat it all. When invited for a meal they may bring the bread—yesterday's, stolen, homemade—or else they'll bring a poem to read, a flower (a single cobra lily, water lily or lotus pod—never roses), Mardi Gras beads, lottery tickets, a wrought-iron umbrella stand picked up from the curb on the way over—they

---

13. Packages of sugar, salt, pepper, ketchup, mayonnaise and tartar sauce as well as napkins will be appropriated from various cafés, fast-food joints and diners. You don't necessarily need to place an order to visit the condiment station in many establishments. An all-you-can-eat buffet or salad bar isn't limited to just that sitting. Knapsacks, bags, pockets, any receptacle may be discreetly filled. Fruit in particular travels well. A pineapple centerpiece is fair game.

14. From Diane di Prima in *Memoirs of a Beatnik*.

don't like to show up empty-handed. Bohemians have been known to bring large jugs of wine and take what's left of it home with them. Taking back wine from a lover, by the way, might be just the kind of terrible thing that ends the relationship.

Bohemians like a recipe that promises arousal. They have read, with an almost clinical curiosity, *Venus in the Kitchen,* a tiny pink cookbook[15] of aphrodisiacs.

Many of these recipes are surreal, "delectable absurdities," writes the author, which makes it suitable reading for an impromptu poetry salon at the Bohemian household. Bohemians will entertain the idea, at least abstractly, of eating "marrow of leopard." This clearly is not a popular book with vegans, who are both the most and least imaginative of Bohemians. Vegans are equally disapproving of the cookbooks by Alice B. Toklas and Salvador Dalí, though they cannot help but be amused by the illustrations in Dalí's book, especially the one of the dwarf with a toadstool hat and Priapus-sized erection upon which is balanced a black-eyed pea. Bohemians, even vegans, are never prudish.

All Bohemians are easily distracted while cooking. The impulse to write a haiku while chopping a green pepper, the urge to improvise a dance when a favorite piece of music is played, a telephone call from overseas, a call concerning a political issue or picking up a book or newspaper may result in burning the chickpeas that soaked for two days, pasta boiled until mush, chicken necks reduced to a gelatinous goo.

15. Existentialist author Graham Greene, who wrote the introduction to this book, calls the collection of aphrodisiacs unserious and shameless.

Bohemian Dining Manifesto

1.   *If the Bohemian is saving money:* Bohemians don't mind cooking at their place. They will invite friends with dramatic, gregarious, opinionated and contradictory natures, so look out! Occasionally they make adventuresome dishes such as Spam and oyster casserole and serve it with a bottle of Amarone that they have been cherishing, a gift from an uncle. They will expect you to bring bread or more wine, any wine as long as it's not from California. Bohemians don't like California wine since it is a poor imitation of French Bordeaux.

2.   *If eating out is out of the question:* There is always coffee at coffee shops and cafés. Diners with a hard-core waitstaff are first choice because of the bottomless cup. Bohemians' second choice when they have a lot of writing to do and can't bear to work alone at home any longer, possibly because there is no heat, will be the café with overstuffed chairs and furniture (none of which will match). A fireplace, especially in San Francisco, is desirable.

3.   *If the Bohemian finds a hundred-dollar bill on the sidewalk:* Bohemians will take a friend and challenge themselves to have dinner at a pricey Italian restaurant, the kind of place with limos waiting out front. The friend will be persuaded to carry the tip and drinks. It could work.

Lobster is the other kind of food upon which Bohemians may splurge. The first thing Bohemians will do when the lobster arrives—if familiar with Dalí's "Lobster Telephone"—is hold the lobster up to their ear and say "Hello?" Pause. "It's for you." No one else, except the waiter who is in art school, will get this.

4.   *If the Bohemian is eating out:* The Bohemian rarely eats American food in restaurants, preferring to buck the American globalization trend in deference to authentic cultures elsewhere. As a matter of fact, now more than ever, Bohemians eat Middle Eastern food as much as possible. They are always somewhat contrary. Contenders include: Indian, Ethiopian (only the authentic kind of place where you eat with your hands), Senegalese, Vietnamese, Korean, Japanese, Chinese, Moroccan, Armenian, Albanian, Mexican, macrobiotic and Ukrainian. Greek diners are a staple, and then there's the occasional Dutch or Portuguese or Austrian restaurant. Restaurants with names like Noodle Town, Grand Sechuan, Salam, Khyber Pass, Lupes and Africa all figure in. Other considerations: establishments that serve inexpensive alcohol. These include taverns and bars, both known, like the Cedar Tavern, and unknown holes-in-the-wall.

5.   *If the Bohemian wins the lottery or sells a novel:* Bohemians will take five friends to a Japanese Peruvian restaurant in TriBeCa and pay for the surrounding tables to be empty so that no yuppies will be seated next to them. They will order several bottles of wine. They prefer Burgundy and will start with, perhaps, a 1959 La Tache. The Bordeaux Petrus 1961 will be on the table, too. They will order the best Champagne and by the end of the evening drink out of the bottle, which will be passed around.

   If the Bohemian's fantasy restaurant is hard to get into, possibly because the Bohemian has neglected to make a reservation or because some of the friends are still wearing their mime makeup and clown outfits, they will take a taxi to another fancy restaurant and try again.

6.   *If you're paying:* Bohemians will eat anywhere.

SPECIFIC DIETARY NOTES

BEAT. Meals are often an inconvenience. They get in the way of jamming, poetry, painting, writing, driving. (Beef jerky is viewed as a nutritional behind-the-wheel meal.) The quicker the better. A pouch of ramen noodles in boiling water, a Swanson turkey potpie in the oven for twenty minutes. (Both, incidentally, are three for a dollar; this is not overlooked.) Of course, there are times when a meal will be celebrated with friends. This is when projects are completed—the novel finished, the chapbook published, etc. A communal table will erupt almost spontaneously. This is strictly potluck.

GYPSY/FAIRY FOLK/HIPPIE. The real down-to-earth types will undoubtedly have a smokehouse. Here they will smoke the trout and salmon they have personally caught. It ends with fish, however. No Bohemian is prepared to down a deer or wild turkey. They're more likely to invite them into the house. First of all, Bohemians don't own hunting weapons, and then there's the issue of the hunting license. Chances are they don't have a driver's license or marriage license, either. When living on the land, Gypsy Bohemians may grow their own vegetables and milk their own goats for cheese, yogurt, etc. Goats will take road trips with the Bohemian and generally sit in the backseat.

ZEN. Many Zen Bohemians are vegans. Sensitive to the discomfort and ethics of animal labor, they would never eat honey after all the hard work the bees went through to produce it; after all, it takes more than 150 trips to flowers to make one teaspoon of honey. Imagination in the kitchen is a must if you are going to cook with tofu, basmati rice and shiitake mushrooms as core ingredients. Because they often drink alcohol, other Bohemians don't mind hav-

ing the Zens around. All Zens are well versed in tea—to which they may add rice milk, soy milk or oat milk.

DANDY. Culinary implements are as important as art supplies. The Dandy is sure to have a cherry pitter, lemon zester, oyster shucker, whisks of various sizes, parchment paper, not to mention a diverse arsenal of spices ranging from galangale and hyssop (medieval) to garam masala and asafoetida (Indian). Other standard supplies include star anise (also used medicinally, specifically for lung ailments), cloves (cooking and toothaches) and lavender honey. All Dandy Bohemians have orange blossom water, which they will splash into their coffee.

NOUVEAU. They host dinner parties—always catered. They take artists to brunch. In short, they pick up the tab. They take cooking classes: Indian cuisine, the tandoori kitchen, edible flowers, ayurvedic recipes, ancient Greek and Roman cooking. They will own all sorts of appliances from food processors to rice makers to bread makers but will not have used any of them more than once.

Cookbooks, the Short List

The Best of Lord Krishna's Cuisine

The Ayurvedic Cookbook

The Little Book of Indian Recipes

Rose Recipes from Olden Times

Fabulous Feasts: Medieval Cookery and Ceremony

To the King's Taste: Richard II's Book of Feasts and Recipes Adapted for Modern Cooking

Venus in the Kitchen, or Love's Cookery Book

The Alice B. Toklas Cook Book

The Moosewood Cookbook

Les Diners de Gala by Salvador Dalí (out of print and expensive; this might have to be a gift)

The Twenty-four-Hour Menu of the Starving Bohemian

Midnight.   Between sets. Two beers, on the house, for being in the band.

4:00 a.m.   Arrive home from gig. Pint of coffee ice cream from twenty-four-hour deli across the street purchased on last trip from lugging amp and instrument up four-story walk-up.

10:00 a.m. Wake up. Already one hour late for temp job at law firm. For breakfast, eat fortune cookie that's been sitting on counter for a few days.

10:45 a.m. Arrive at work. Back-to-back cups of black coffee from office kitchen.

Noon.   Lunch. One individual-size liqueur-soaked (Kahlua or Amaretto) bundt cake lifted from carton in conference room. (One of the partners invested in a baking concern and sends said cakes to clients.)

3:15 p.m. Several Perugina chocolates that a secretary received from a boyfriend.

4:00 p.m. Still at work. More coffee.

5:30 p.m.   En route to apartment after work. Walk through
            neighborhood gourmet market and try all the free
            food samples: andouille sausage, smoked mozzarella,
            fois gras on toast, asparagus spears sautéed in garlic
            and balsamic vinegar.

6:00 p.m.   Arrive home. Several swigs of chilled water kept in
            the fridge in an apple juice jar.

6:30 p.m.   Wake from nap. Roommate/bandmate makes
            dinner—grilled cheese sandwiches—with an iron
            and aluminum foil.

8:00 p.m.   Rehearsal. Iced-tea and candy bar.

10:15 p.m. Post-rehearsal at Rudy's Bar & Grill. One can of beer
            and two free hot dogs with ketchup. (Cheap beer and
            free dogs make this a mainstay for NYC Bohemians.)

11:55 p.m. Home. Ice cream sandwich won in poker game with
            roommates.

BOHEMIAN SHELTER
AND SET DESIGN

The SPLENDOR of DECADENCE

Bohemians revolt against depersonalized and sanitized environments: pristine puritanical lofts polished to a gleam and stripped of quirks, clutter and mess. They are not interested in tidying up their corners and tables and shelves burgeoning with scraps of ideas, paints, inks from France and glass pens from Italy, flea market silver, poetry journals, sculpture, pottery, stones, skulls, shells, taxidermy squirrels and spiderwebs.

Bohemians live any- and everywhere. Bohemian shelter may be your place, for example, because when Bohemians come to visit they may end up staying a long, long time. Bohemians will live out of boxes, make furniture out of boxes, hell, they'll sleep in them. Bohemians with no discernible income can furnish an apartment like a prince down on his luck, the maid on permanent leave. Bohemians adore the idea of the ephemeral home whether it's a houseboat, A-frame or Airstream. Bohemians camp out in abandoned buildings, put up their charcoal sketches, hang their canvases from the ceiling as room dividers and fill the floor with votive candles. Bohemians may receive their mail at a café or bar.

Thirteen Things You Will Never Find in a Bohemian Home

1. magazine rack in bathroom

2. mousetraps of any kind

3. calculator

4. thermometer (They know when they have a fever.)

5. smoke detector

6. microwave

7. treadmill, stationary bicycle, etc.

8. electric knife

9. electric blanket

10. lazy Susan

11. artificial flowers in plastic or silk

12. padded toilet seat cover

13. self-tanner of any kind

Nouveau Shelter and Set Design

Nouveaus are not ashamed to have a posh Fifth Avenue address or a villa in Florence. But they may, swept up in the Bohemian spirit, move to a loft, top floor, in a down-and-out, up-and-coming neighborhood like Williamsburg or DUMBO or Red Hook in Brooklyn, though they'll insist upon an elevator. They may buy a building in the historically Bohemian thirteenth arrondissement or the grittier Montreuil in Paris or a gigantic space in Berlin's Prenzlauer Berg district. They could even end up living on a houseboat. They can handle the ebb and flow, pitch and roll—they learned on yachts.

Nouveau Bohemians also favor large farmhouses, cabins (never as a primary residence), ranches in Taos and tumbling castles that they will restore as a sort of artist's retreat. Nouveaus will also pick up and move to foreign cities, taking over several suites in the most luxurious hotel. The Nouveau extends invitations to Bohemians to talk, drink, make music, develop ideas, patents and formulas and finish their manuscripts.[16]

The Nouveau doesn't need to barter a painting to buy an appliance or overstuffed chair. Nouveaus can afford an interior decorator but don't. If they can't find the desired object at a flea market or auction, they have it custom-made. This, of course, keeps artisans employed.

16. In 1913, Mabel Dodge, a socialite heiress turned Nouveau Bohemian, transformed her lower Fifth Avenue home in Greenwich Village into a celebrated salon filled with political, sexual and artistic rebels—America's radical intelligentsia. Ten years later, Mabel moved to Taos, New Mexico, divorced and married a Pueblo Indian (Tony Luhan) and soon created a "Village West" offering temporary sanctuary to Willa Cather, Mary Austin, Leon Gaspard, Ansel Adams, Georgia O'Keeffe and D. H. Lawrence, among others. (When Thomas Wolfe, author of *Look Homeward, Angel,* rolled in totally smashed with two prostitutes, he was shown the road. Mabel's tolerance for Bohemianism had its limits.)

The Nouveau will paint murals over the fireplace and on the walls and ask artist friends to visit and paint in exchange for free lodging. There is always at least one guest room with a private bath. Nouveau shelters swell with the photographs, paintings and sculptures of Bohemian friends and acquaintances. They buy their friends' books twenty at a time and have them autographed for gifts.

The Nouveau may be an actor, and after years of only minor parts and fruitless auditions—a pizza or feminine hygiene commercial, or worse, something promoting an SUV is out of the question—buy their own theater company. So there.

There is always plenty of crystal stemware, brought out for literary salons, political discussions, gigs, readings and costume parties that start in the sitting or living room and end up spreading throughout every room, from the kitchen to the bath. The maid does not look forward to cleaning up after these soirées.

Gypsy Shelter and Set Design

The wanderlust of the Gypsy means the home, at some point in time, may have wheels: a van, a VW bus, school bus, wagon, caravan. (See Wheels.) This may be explained by the Gypsy need for freedom. The houseboat, precursor to the VW van, is also a natural lodging of the Gypsy as it has appeal to every kind of Bohemian.

Like the Zen Bohemian, the Gypsy understands the ephemeral quality of possessions and dwellings.

This, however, does not mean the Gypsy is immune to the idea of non-mobile dwellings. Farmhouses, barns, coach houses, abandoned airplanes, even tree houses are favorites. When Gypsy Bohemians drop by, invited or not, they may stay for days, months, even years and also entertain guests who stay for days, months and even years.[17]

Gypsies always put a personal stamp on the living space.

Decoration! Patterns! Cultural mélange! The rug of even the most unglamorous flat, bus or caravan may be Persian—there may

---

17. In August 1911, English artist Augustus John and Dorelia rented a pink bungalow on sixty acres of sprawling, woodsy land. They showed up with their children in a colorful caravan of carts and wagons and turned the place into the quintessential Bohemian commune. The coach house was converted into a studio, the cottage accommodated the seemingly endless stream of visitors, some invited, some who just dropped in. Other guests stayed in the gypsy caravans parked all over the place. Of course there were parties on weekends—in gypsy tents.

be several of different sizes layered across the floor, or one that's too large that is allowed to curl up the wall—and the lighting will have the aura of candlelight, probably because, if there is electricity, an Indian scarf has been thrown over the shade. Gypsy lamps include hanging mosque lamps, Turkish lamps, lanterns and oil lamps.

Batik and/or Indian bedspreads and other fabrics collected from travels abroad will be found on walls, on ceilings, on beds, as mosquito netting around the bed. There will be a minimum of one embroidered piano shawl with fringe that will, when not being worn, be in one of the following three places: tacked over the window in the bathroom, draped over a table or tossed over the shade of a floor lamp. There may be several cushions in various patterns on the floor and a low coffee table of brass from India.

The birdcages are purely decorative. And yes, there will be beaded curtains in doorways.

Beat Shelter and Set Design

Beats generally live above or underneath something: apartments, basements, attics, top floors,[18] in cars occasionally, with friends and lovers, in warehouses, in the back of bookstores,[19] SROs, cheap motels and hotels—historically speaking, Hotel Chelsea in New York, the Chateau Marmont in Hollywood, and since the Swiss American in San Francisco is long gone, Hotel Bohème, and the now extinct Beat hotel at 9, rue Git-le-Coeur, a down-and-out rooming house with shared hole-in-the-floor toilets. Beats will also squat in buildings and with relatives, usually an aunt, until they get the itch to travel or are asked to leave.

Heat and hot water are considered luxuries, and many Bohemians have burned furniture—Diane di Prima recalls that friends would bring six-by-six beams, doors and furniture to saw up on the living room floor for the fireplace—and even manuscripts ("My passionate drama will warm us," sings Rodolfo in Puccini's *La Bohème*) in a pinch.

Availability of hot water and electricity has little influence over the Beat's choice of habitat. Lighting will consist of candles in wine bottles—Chianti is traditional—naked bulbs dangling from the ceiling and lamps from the flea market or street. Mosque lamps, Indian stars and paper lanterns end up in Beat pads from time to time, after travels or given as gifts by the wanderlustful friend who spilled not one but two bottles of wine on the sofa bed. Beats are

---

18. Anaïs Nin describes the Morton Street apartment of filmmakers Maya Deren and Alexander Hammid: "We arrived at her studio in the Village, a vast place on the top floor. It was filled with exotic objects: drums, masks, statues, recordings, cameras, lights, screens, costumes."

19. Diane di Prima, author of *Memoirs of a Beatnik,* was living in Washington Square Park when she was offered a live-in job running a bookshop on MacDougal Street.

not shy about sharing their bed with three
or four people at a time. Sheets and pillowcases, yes; bedspreads, no. Blankets if
they're lucky. The bed is always rumpled.
Beats are free spirits, earthy, in touch with
their animal nature. Beats will be sexually
intimate with more than one person in the
bed on a given night.

The bathtub is usually in the kitchen.

Beats let just about anyone stay in their apartment. A Beat
about to take the Greyhound to Chicago for the holidays may give
the keys to his apartment to the homeless musician encountered
daily on the subway. Naturally, there's going to be some fallout.

Beats leave the place they move into pretty much as is. No
painting, ever. They tack or tape up charcoal sketches of nudes and
photos of friends and hang paintings where nails already exist. If
furniture is required it's found on the street or at the Salvation
Army. Beats also build with found or existing materials. Milk crates
and police and construction barricades (bed frame), cinder blocks
(bookshelves), cable spool (occasional table or nightstand). Chairs
may be "recaned" with bicycle tire inner tubes. (See Nine Bohemian
Case Studies—Cody.)

If they have been in the dwelling more than six months, there's
bound to be some tribal art: carved African masks and figurines, a
Buddha and assorted Hindu statuettes, especially Ganesh.

There will always be some means of making music in the Beat
dwelling. A record player, guitar, banjo, trumpet, conga drums,
bongos, flute, upright bass, an accordion. At the very least, a harmonica in middle C, although there could be several in minor keys.
The Beat can handle moody downswings better than any other
Bohemian, as long as there is a bottle of wine, a pen and a notebook.

Zen Shelter and Set Design

The Zen Bohemian is comfortable with both solitude and communal living situations. Ashrams, monasteries, youth hostels, tents, communes, attics, chicken coops, A-frames in the wilderness, even trees are suitable temporary digs. After all, isn't all of life temporary? Zen Bohemians also understand that no one ever owns anything, that ownership is an illusion. They are not ruled by a desire for creature comforts.

Zens may live and work in their studio, but even if the space is monastic, they create splendor in their minds. The Zen finds the idea of global consciousness a bit limited and is more interested in intergalactic consciousness, which explains the telescope.

No other Bohemian fares better sleeping on hard surfaces, whether it's outdoors—on the beach, for example—or on a dirt floor in a hut. Often the Zen Bohemian bed has little more give than a yoga mat (also suitable for sleeping on). The sleeping bag figures in, as do hammocks, futons, foam or an inflatable mattress on the floor. (A sleeping bag under the stars is more glamorous to the Zen than a loft in TriBeCa.) When the Zen does have a bed, the bedspread in cooler weather will consist of said sleeping bag if it is the kind that unzips.

In the summer, there will be an Indian bedspread.

Zens do not go in for ornamentation and worldly possessions. They may or may not have chairs or other furniture outside of orange crates for storing books. A small Buddha, a little Kali, Krishna or Laxhmi figurine, incense burner, shrine, candlesticks and record player or cassette player and saris or plain canvas for curtains may be the sole embellishments. Cooking is generally limited to what can be prepared on a Coleman camping stove—that way they are not beholden to the local power company—Bunsen burner or hot plate.

Mugs and plates will be stoneware, handmade on a potter's wheel, or enamelware. Zens often have a collapsible cup left over from camping.

Lighting consists of kerosene lamps, halogen lamps, full-spectrum lightbulbs, salt lamps (favored because they emit negative ions), flashlights and candles. Zens usually have straw mats and a few prayer rugs, rarely Oriental carpets or kilims unless purchased directly in the country in which they were made, and they will never own an animal skin rug. Zens always ask you to remove your shoes when you come in.

Zens are the most outdoorsy of the Bohemians and are the most likely to have gardens. They will pay as much attention to the rocks as to the plants.

Dandy Shelter and Set Design

The Dandy Bohemian has style unhindered by financial limitations. You get the feeling that if the Bohemian had all the money in the world, the living room, studio, loft, flat, etc., would still have the same eclectic mien. There's a threadbare old-money quality to many Bohemian homes—the look of an aristocrat who's fallen upon hard times or taken a cavalier attitude to upkeep as if there are more important things to think about than refurbishing and dusting. The Bohemian home may have a decadent squalor that is lavish, never too kempt, pristine, cold, shiny or new. Dandies have the imagination to see aesthetic value and emotional beauty in objects, textiles and furniture that are out of fashion or considered useless by the label-conscious bourgeoisie. The Dandy household is "always in a state of delicate equilibrium between threadbare poetic freedom and aristocratic elegance."[20]

Furniture may have been culled from flea markets, streets, country roads, estate auctions and deceased relatives. It may be painted, gilded, distressed, re-covered, in short, personalized. Splendid surroundings suit Dandies. For Dandy Bohemians, all life's a stage, and they are the set designers. They may use foreign newspapers (especially in languages not using the Roman alphabet, such as Chinese, Greek and Arabic) as wallpaper in the bathroom. Never content with hideous linoleum, they may tear the pages out of Gibbon's *The Decline and Fall of the Roman Empire* and varnish them to the floor, creating a tile effect. Cracked walls and crumbling plaster are left as is—after all, even modern-day aristocrats can't afford the upkeep on their manor houses. Dandies may name

---

20. Mina Loy's son-in-law describing her home, in *Becoming Modern, The Life of Mina Loy,* by Carolyn Burke.

rooms to match usage or décor: the Gentleman's Lounge, the Yellow Room, *la Salle Sauvage,* the Dutch Kitchen.

Taxidermy is a perennial favorite of the Dandy Bohemian, as it harkens back to the nineteenth-century age of scientific discovery. Taxidermy, too, is viewed as maintenance-free pets.[21]

Baudelaire had a room, according to the journalist Maxime Rude, "hung with black, and with stuffed crocodiles and serpents brought back from the Tropics, which seemed to writhe about under the high ceiling."

The smallest carriage house, the most ruinous castle would be preferable to a cozy caravan, dingy six-floor walk-up, enormous basement, big barn or VW bus. Dandies desire a dwelling as flamboyant as their dress. Something perhaps with historic or cultural significance. They'd love to move into a defunct lighthouse, windmill or an old bank.[22] If they do live in a small apartment, they never call it a studio, it is always a pied-à-terre.

If a Dandy did happen to have grounds or a lawn, there would be peacocks. And if a lake, swans.

21. Writer Alexander Dumas tells us that Jean Gérard, better known as Grandville, furnished his garret near the Palais des Beaux-Arts with a stuffed squirrel playing the flute and "a gull which hung from the ceiling with its wings outstretched, looking as though it still skimmed the waves."

22. Dandy painters Messrs. David McDermott and Peter McGough chose a classic old bank as their New York City dwelling.

The Bohemian Bathroom

Bohemians live in a world with few inhibitions. Therefore, Bohemian bathrooms rarely have locks. Sometimes the door does not close all the way or may close with a small hook.

Some bathrooms have an Indian bedspread, sari or other fabric on rings instead of a door unless the bathroom doubles as a darkroom, in which case there will actually be a door that, with a good yank, closes snugly.

The bathtub, if it is in the bathroom and not in the kitchen, will be of the cast iron, claw-footed variety. If not originally in the flat, it will have been found at the dump or on the street—several friends helped carry it up to the fifth floor, after which they were rewarded with a bottle of wine. Or the Bohemian has made the tub, usually of wood that is polyurethaned, or possibly of tiles like the ones on the tub the Bohemian had while living in Mexico, the place with the scorpions.

A lot goes on in the Bohemian bathtub. Tie-dyeing, along with dyeing garments in general. A bucket with a plunger serves as the Bohemian washing machine. Photographers may tint photographs there with tea, coffee, selenium, etc. Other uses include temporary housing of rescued reptiles and amphibians, dishwashing, clothes washing, bathing, reading, writing, sex and suicide.

Mirrors will be anything with a hand-painted frame from India or Morocco to an ornate Venetian mirror from a flea market or a giant piece of broken mirror. Assorted bead, shell and coral necklaces will hang from the mirror; otherwise they hang from a hook left on the wall by the previous tenant.

Other things you will find in the bathroom include small hand-painted wooden boxes from Kashmir for earrings, nose rings, etc.; an antique Bakelite bobby pin container; and a dented, tarnished silver-plate shaving cup containing a hairbrush and wayward paint-brushes that double as makeup brushes; antique apothecary jars, especially if they contained belladonna or leeches; towels from assorted hotels and a nude sculpture with outstretched arm. The toilet paper roll goes here.

The medicine cabinet is usually whatever was in place when the Bohemians moved in, a vintage medical cupboard or something they have made themselves. Poems and photographs will be taped to the inside.

It is of no use to ask Bohemians what brands they prefer. Bohemians might be able to recall in detail the image on a tube of toothpaste or hair pomade or describe a scent or color with a haiku. They will be able to tell you about the shop in Paris or London or Florence or San Francisco where they bought the little tube, jar or bottle of something pertaining to beauty or hygiene. But it is necessary to scout the bathroom yourself to determine brands, as the Bohemian will not remember the names. Like the Bohemian pet, toothpastes are generally exotic. You might find Kingfisher toothpaste (the Bohemian appreciates a toothpaste that shares a name with a beer from India), Auromere Herbal, XyliBrush, Elgydium, etc. The Dandy uses Marvis (Italian) in aquatic mint, ginger mint or jasmine mint. Thea Osato, a Bohemian artist in Baltimore, says brushing with Italian toothpaste gives her a fleeting taste of Italy and makes brushing less unpleasant.

The Bohemian may also use homeopathic toothpaste, such as Homeodent in anise or lemon. Never Aquafresh, Colgate or Crest.

Chances are there is no deodorant in the Bohemian bathroom. If there is, it will be either a rock crystal or something else from the health food store, or something wildly toxic and powerful. This will have been given to the Bohemian by a relative and will never be opened.

WHAT'S ON THE SHELVES

SESAME OIL	*For full-body massages (an ayurvedic daily ritual).*
TIGER BALM	*For sore muscles after carrying amplifier, upright bass or drums to fourth- or fifth-floor walk-up. Also used after night of wheat-pasting posters around town to announce opening, reading or performance, helping friends move, etc.*
MONKEY BRAND BLACK TOOTH POWDER	*This was purchased for decorative reasons but may be used by visiting friends.*
TOOTHBRUSH	*One only. May be shared with lover, roommate and guests.*
LAVENDER OIL	*Used as a perfume, salve for burns and headache relief.*
DR. BRONNER'S 18-IN-1 MAGIC SOAP	*(pure castile, liquid variety) Used for hair, body, hand laundry and sculpture projects with plaster.*
HENNA	*For hair coloring, hand, foot and face decoration.*
CARMEX	*In the bathroom from April through September. Otherwise it's carried around in the pocket of an over-coat. The Bohemian sees it as cold-sore prevention; who knows how many people he or she made out with the other night at that club.*
GIANT SEA SPONGE OR LOOFAH	*A washcloth is out of the question.*
YERBA PRIMA SKIN BRUSH	*For dry skin brushing, part of the Bohemian healthcare program.*
STRAIGHT RAZOR	*For the edges around the goatee and shaping sideburns.*
MOUSTACHE WAX	*It seemed like a good idea at the time.*
BAG BALM	*Turpentine is rough on an artist's hands.*
LATTE PER IL CORPO BY S.M. NOVELLA	*Picked up while in Florence or at Aedes de Venustas on Christopher Street in New York City.*
ENCHANTED OILS	*These will include Lucky Dog, Success and Morgan's Fairie Dance.*
GOLDENSEAL DROPS	*Used as an antibiotic.*

ASSORTED BACH FLOWER REMEDIES	*Cheaper than seeing an analyst. The Bohemian is sure they'd work but never remembers to take them.*
CALAMINE LOTION	*For bites of assorted insects encountered camping, at youth hostels, cheap hotels, etc.*
VEGENIN	*They stock up on this and other over-the-counter remedies containing codeine when in Europe.*
A DOLL LEG OR HEAD	*This washed up on the beach and seemed to speak of the lost soul of humanity and of broken dreams.*
A SMALL BUDDHA	*If not a gift, this will have been purchased in Cambodia, Japan, China, Chinatown or at a flea market. This does not mean the Bohemian is a Buddhist.*
TWEEZERS	*These may have been left in another room after a splinter was removed (the dangerous floors have not been sanded in years. A baby could be impaled on rotting shards of wood. Even the cat treads lightly). Also used to replace stones in flea-market jewelry.*

Animals may also be muses for the Bohemian. Björk wore a dress inspired by a swan to the Academy Awards in 2001. The press dismissed it as if it were the ugly duckling of gowns. Nouveau Bohemian and pop phenomenon Edie Sedgwick made tender sketches of mice and raccoons—hardly typical house pets. Guillaume Apollinaire in 1920 published *Le Bestiaire ou Cortège d'Orphée,* a collection of poems inspired by animals—lobster, cat and camel, to name a few. He even paid homage to insects with lyrics about the fly, grasshopper and flea. Louis Durey, a friend of Jean Cocteau's, set these poems to music.

Of all the odes to a pest, however, Franz Kafka tops the list with his story, "The Metamorphosis," in which Gregor Samsa turns into a giant cockroach and spends most of his time hanging out under a couch wondering what his father and boss will think of his new appearance.

Edgar Allan Poe—well, there's "The Raven," of course, but Poe also edited and lent his name to an academic book entitled *The Conchologist's First Book,* published in 1837. It was the first book to discuss the shells of mollusks as well as the animals that lived within. It was also the only one of Poe's books to go into a second printing during his lifetime.

William Blake was moved by a "tyger, tyger, burning bright," and in *Les Fleurs du Mal* Charles Baudelaire poured his pathos into the albatross, declaring "The Poet is like this monarch of the clouds. . . . Exiled on earth amidst its hooting crowds."

Many pages could be devoted to the cat as the quintessential Bohemian pet. Fortune 500 types never have them. Cats are too aloof, too sexy, too independent, and will not fetch or heel. They will not tolerate baths or having their claws clipped. They navigate nimbly the mantels, counters and tables between tall, fragile things and feign to have no understanding of "no trespassing." In his poem perhaps purchased from a South Asian or South American market, in a pocket or under a coat. It should be understood that the Bohemian will never confine the bootleg animal in luggage where it might suffocate, be exposed to X-rays or be stowed in a non-pressurized cargo hold.

Bohemians explore their own animal natures with animals. Animals may also populate their fantasy lifestyle. Augustus John, with his Gypsy passion, acquired all the trappings for getting back to the land: cows, a breeding herd of saddleback pigs, various donkeys, New Forest ponies, cart horses, miscellaneous cats and dogs, twelve hives of bees that stung everyone who took a nature walk, a dovecote from which all the doves flew away and a biteful monkey.

For the most part, however, Bohemians do not expect their animals to do a job or a trick, fetch a newspaper or slippers, run down a fox or wade into marshes to retrieve a duck shot from an early blue sky, etc., unless, perhaps, they are traveling with a dancing bear—a Gypsy Bohemian fixture—or monkey and said animal can help out in an entertaining fashion. Doves, of course, are another matter, as every magician needs a few to disappear and reappear from a top hat or silk handkerchief.

Bohemians never send their pets to obedience school, never train them to attack or bite on command. Bohemians leave that entirely up to their pets. If they themselves are bitten or scratched they assume responsibility and recognize there is a language barrier. They ask themselves what they have done to distress the animal. They never consider discipline. They do not show their animals or send them to grooming salons—though they might braid their pet's hair—or tamper with their anatomy. No declawing, tooth extractions, tail bobbing, wing clipping or ear straightening. Bohemians have, however, studied carefully the paintings and sculptures of the ancient Egyptians and have whimsically considered for a minute or two piercing their cats' ears.

Bohemians may consider the pet as live plumage, a breathing, blinking, decorative entity draped around their neck, perched on the shoulder or nestled in a pocket—a weasel, marmoset, sugar glider or cockatoo, a feral embellishment more adorable than a dead fox stole. While the Bohemian may poke a feather into a hat or a buttonhole, many know that a colorful parrot carried on the shoulder is more charming, particularly if it knows equally colorful language.

While technically flora, the Bohemian's ideal pet is a Venus's-flytrap. They appreciate a pet that can feed itself.

AFFAIRS OF THE HEART

Bohemian Love

If you're looking for conventional love, skip this chapter. There's passion, romance, trysts, affairs, unrequited loves, infidelities, sleeping around, longing, thwarted love and suicides.

Bohemians fall in love with their muses. Platonically, romantically, physically. Because they are so egotistically romantic, Bohemians, at least in the beginning, can't discriminate between love and lust. They cannot, in fact, discriminate between love and art. This gives the muse a lot of responsibility.

It is the job of the muse to inspire, provoke, evoke, invoke, tantalize. It is the job of the muse to be an icon of possibility. Senses are sharpened, heightened around the muse. Wit, words, shapes, colors, lines, forms, fabrics—everything is draped over the silhouette of promise and illusion when the muse is around. The muse on the crest, the edge of the actual affair, the potential of the affair, at the beginning of the affair, holds more reflected light—and it will be reflected since it's the Bohemian's perception, never the genuine person—than a full moon or a cathedral full of candles.

The muse may be enchanted with the idea of igniting poetry, architectural monuments and eloquent dialogue. Muses may feel significant posing for paintings, statues and photographs, the chilled studio air dappling their skin in waves reminding them viscerally of the important contribution they are making to art. Many nudes, stories, poems and songs later, however, the muse may start to fade and a new muse will enter the picture. Either that or the muse will find a new Bohemian, or maybe several Bohemians, to enchant. Ditched by the muse, the Bohemian sinks into a deep, dark, self-centered despondency. Bohemians will express melancholy by self-medicating until they find a means of exploiting this emotion.

Unrequited love, unhappy endings, unbemused muses are equally inspirational to the Bohemian whose best poetry, plays, paintings and songs are often based on disappointment.

Open marriages, broken marriages, ménages à trois,[28] a bed full of Bohemians on a frosty night, anything can happen, and the heart may or may not be in it. Intimate and romantic encounters will undoubtedly end up in memoirs, poems, novels and paintings. Never sleep with a Bohemian unless you're willing to have it end up in the public domain.

---

28. Augustus John had a love life as tumultuous as his artistic career. Three years after marrying Ida he fell in love with an artists' model, Dorothy McNeill, known as Dorelia. Dorelia became part of a ménage à trois with Augustus and his wife. They had several children and lived together quite amicably.

Bohemian courtship does not include expensive candlelight dinners, though candles may figure into the picture whether or not there is electricity, especially if a homemade dinner is involved. (See Counterculture Cuisine.)

Bohemians meet lovers at the following places: cafés, bars, peace rallies and/or protest marches, at the pyramids in Cairo during the scorching day, not during the light show (the poet will be talking to a man with a camel), in the checkout line at the grocery store with a flyer to come see a gig or play, at a figure drawing class (they fall for other students, the teacher and the model), art openings, rent parties, costume parties, flea markets, over Champagne during intermission at the opera, theater rehearsals, poetry readings, on subways, trains and buses, at yoga class, qigong class, in Cambodia while photographing temples, in India while photographing monkeys, at the home of a friend (they often fall for their friend's significant other and expect you to understand), etc.

Language may be eighty percent of the Bohemian seduction. Bohemians will memorize long passages from prose poems and lines from E. E. Cummings and Rimbaud and when they toast the object of their desire, they will say something like, "O eternal soul, fulfill thy promise despite the nights alone and the days on fire." They will talk you into love with philosophy, discourses on things ephemeral, physical and metaphysical, their vision of the world, their inventions, their questions. A Bohemian in love will send poems, watercolors and love letters without a single cliché. These may be typed and go on and on in a flurried rapture that sweeps you in, or they may be short and seductively scrawled on the back of a cigarette box. (See Stationery, Calling Cards, etc.) They may embellish the envelopes, slip letters impatiently under your door, leave flowers plucked from a window box on your doorstep or have extravagant flowers sent by a florist and eat nothing but fortune cookies for a week. They will ask the object of love/desire to model for them, appear in their independent film or do the reading of the screenplay they've just written.

Bohemians in love will knit you a strange sweater, customize your shoes with metallic paint, cut your hair, blindfold you and take you to a club where a chanteuse you've been mooning over is singing, bring you a slightly shredded Victorian fan in emerald green or a pen box from the flea market or a monkey skull in a hand-carved box or a book they found in the trash room of their building, which may be where they have gotten most of their furniture. From their window on the top floor they will toss you the keys wrapped in a black silk stocking or lace bra or garter belt scented with Chanel's Russian Leather or Caron Pour un Homme left by their last lover, or an extinct perfume like Septième Sens or My Sin, a different black item each time you visit. They will play songs on their guitar and sing, and better yet, they will write songs about you that describe you in a peculiar though positive light. Bohemians in love will take you to their favorite haunts and dim underground places and bars on barges and in basements. Bohemians in love expect you to forgive their lack of heat and hot water and to happily trek downstairs or down the hall to the communal toilet. The Bohemian in love expects you to be unconcerned that the bed in their studio is shared by an artist who paints all night, to understand that these circumstances are glamorous because they are temporary, a result of living a truthful, uncompromised life.

Many Bohemians are dedicated to liberty and often overlook jealousy. Needless to say, this can get tricky.[29]

---

29. Neal Cassady was sleeping with Allen Ginsberg and shared his wife with Jack Kerouac, who was far more in love with Neal.

While a Bohemian may have a preference for one sex above another, Bohemians are usually open when it comes to exploration. George Sand, Frida Kahlo and Virginia Woolf were not immune to the feminine mystique.

Jack Kerouac, Paul Verlaine and William Burroughs[30] were not immune to the masculine mystique. Allen Ginsberg was definitely a man's man, though in a pinch he could take a roll in the hay with a dame.

Some Bohemians are steadfast in their preference for one gender above the other. Picasso loved women. Lots of women. Gertrude Stein was a one-woman woman.

Bohemians are immune to taboos regarding age difference. Anaïs Nin was oblivious to the age of her lovers, as was the artist Georgia O'Keeffe. Ten, twenty, thirty years younger? No problem.

Thwarted Love

Since they generally live on them, top floors often figure into Bohemian love gone wrong. A naked, existentially dejected artist resting her head on the stove in front of a stream of gas in a Greenwich Village walk-up; the lover in bed who, by chance, wakes up in time; a leap from the top floor of a studio in Paris; wrists slashed in a studio bleeding unsuccessfully because the pan of water is too cold; a bit of rope in the garret. Sometimes Bohemians end it all in a cornfield with a bullet, in a seedy alley-

---

30. Jack Kerouac was a ladies' man on paper—three marriages—yet preferred the "glory" of male companionship over women. Poet Paul Verlaine was also conventional on paper, with a sixteen-year-old bride. He ran off with the poet Arthur Rimbaud. William Burroughs and his wife moved to Mexico, where he picked up young men.

way with a noose, or with a drug overdose,[31] very popular with
overthrown and outdated muses, and of course there's always the
old killing themselves slowly method. The traditional substances
are absinthe, whiskey and gin.

Bohemian Weddings

Bohemians have as much disdain for marriage as they do for many
conventional holidays. (Christmas or Hanukkah may be tossed over
for a pagan celebration such as winter solstice.) Even the term
common-law husband or *wife* (they don't like laws, and they are never
common) makes them break into a cold sweat. For many
Bohemians, marriage papers mean the act of commitment is
reported to the government, and the less they know the better.

The very essence of Utopia precludes such banal conventions
as marriage, but since Bohemians are sometimes as romantic and
idealistic as they are cynical, many Bohemians tie the knot.
Bohemians may wed to have an excuse for a big party, not that they
ever need an excuse. A marriage may also occur strictly to con-
found and stun friends and the establishment and to cement a sym-
biotic musedom, e.g., a man and woman marrying as inspired
counterparts but with no heterosexual interest whatsoever.
Bohemians have been known to wed at city hall when in a rush to
avoid some sort of legal fiasco or, if living in the United States, for
health benefits should one of the Bohemians have a job that offers
benefits or to avoid deportation.

---

31. Dante Gabriel Rossetti's wife overdosed on laudanum when she suspected he
had a new muse, a model named Fanny Cornforth. Rossetti placed an unpublished
manuscript of his poetry in her coffin but later, feeling a lot less heartsick with
Fanny around, dug her up and retrieved it.

Bootleg weddings are also popular. Marriage may take place in the Cathedral of Notre Dame, for example, with vows read by a friend in a candlelit recess. This, of course, will be purely ceremonial, unsanctioned by the cathedral and not legally binding. Bohemians also get married in cemeteries, in the woods, on a barge, in ruins. It will not be a location that is strange or unfamiliar to them, but perhaps a place where they have had lunch or visited while traveling. They do not get married skydiving, and unless they are surfers, beaches have become too mainstream for the serious Bohemian. Bohemians never use wedding planners.

Friends will read Sappho, ancient Egyptian love poetry translated by Ezra Pound, Rumi and ancient Chinese poetry. The wedding gown may be an antique corset worn with tulle wrapped around an underskirt of aluminum foil, with the groom in a kilt and the flower girl and ring bearer in angel wings. Or the bride may wear an Indian rose silk skirt with a gold paisley motif; the groom will wear a safari outfit for this one. Outfits made of felt, elaborate brocade and denim also figure in wedding ceremonies. Men may be bridesmaids and women may be best men. Brides and grooms of any sex may wear a tuxedo or gown. This includes nightgowns, something vintage and satin. Music will be provided by the guests and/or bride and groom, groom and groom, etc.

The ring may be an afterthought. Bohemian wedding bands include cigar bands, rings from vending machines, nose rings, an ear stud instead of a ring, large hex nuts, something purchased at a flea market, handmade or from a craftsperson with a table on a street, something taken from a relative's jewelry box.

IV

BOHEMIAN ARTS AND LETTERS

READING MATERIAL

Norman Mailer once said, "I detest a well-plotted novel." This is the Bohemian's credo. Bohemians read anything that has been censored in any and all media (including *Ulysses, Naked Lunch, Tropic of Capricorn, Howl, Candide*), out-of-print books, all the existentialists, especially *Being and Nothingness* by Jean-Paul Sartre, everything by Guy de Maupassant, beat poetry and fiction including Maxwell Bodenheim's *My Life and Loves in Greenwich Village, Complete and Uncensored,* famous titles on anarchy, art books, cosmically inclined and Hippie fiction, philosophy books, highly specialized and/or peculiar cookbooks, occult/New Age books (e.g., the *I Ching, The Crystal Handbook,* assorted palm reading and astrology books), miscellaneous diaries, memoirs, erotica, manifestos, musty hardcover books from an attic or barn chosen for nostalgic reasons, rare antique books of etchings and oversized outdated atlases filled with countries that no longer exist—the Belgian Congo, Siam,

Bechuanaland, East Germany, West Germany, the U.S.S.R. These will be used for collages, wrapping paper, wallpaper, floor coverings and stationery.

Bohemians also enjoy comic books, especially R. Crumb, Harvey Pekar's *American Splendor,* Tony Millionaire's *Sock Monkey* and small/underground imprints like *Goodie.*

Books sold at airports only make it to the Bohemian bookshelf if someone leaves them behind. These will be the first books chosen to prop up the missing chaise leg or to sell at the secondhand bookstore to buy wine or help pay the electric bill.

Bohemians use the following items for bookmarkers: matchbook covers, matches, cigarettes, utility bills, leaves, postcards, receipts, used condom wrappers and tarot cards.

It's dangerous to say what Bohemians read and own because they are very, very opinionated. The short list:

Dictionaries and Reference Books

The Devil's Dictionary by Ambrose Bierce

Ancient Egyptian Grammar

Dictionary of Symbolism by Hans Biedermann

An Esperanto dictionary

A Dictionary of the English Language by Samuel Johnson, unabridged only

Ephemeris

The Egyptian Book of the Dead by E. A. Wallis Budge

Lives of the Artists by Giorgio Vasari

The Kama Sutra of Vatsyayana translated by Sir Richard Burton

The Woman's Encyclopedia of Myths and Secrets by Barbara G. Walker (shoots a hole in most of the historical opinions embraced by the average person)

National Green Pages by Co-op America

Nostradamus: The Complete Prophecies

The Elixirs of Nostradamus (Much grooming advice comes from this book.)

Psilocybin, Magic Mushroom Grower's Guide: A Handbook for Psilocybin Enthusiasts by O. T. Oss, O. N. Oeric, foreword by Terence McKenna

Bohemian Must-Reads

The Communist Manifesto by Karl Marx and Friedrich Engels

Siddhartha by Herman Hesse

Justine by Marquis de Sade

Leaves of Grass by Walt Whitman

Les Fleurs du Mal by Charles Baudelaire

Arthur Rimbaud, complete works

Death in Venice by Thomas Mann

The Stranger by Albert Camus

Nana and *Thérèse Raquin* by Émile Zola

The Metamorphosis by Franz Kafka

Satyricon by Petronius

The Motorcycle Diaries by Che Guevara (not to be confused with *Zen and the Art of Motorcycle Maintenance*)

Notes from Underground, The Idiot (no happy endings here) and *Crime and Punishment* by Fyodor Dostoevsky, take your pick

The Decay of an Angel by Yukio Mishima

The Tale of Genji by Lady Murasaki

Scènes de la Bohème by Henry Murger (a merry acceptance of poverty—good luck finding it)

The Alexandria Quartet by Lawrence Durrell

Les Misèrables by Victor Hugo

Story of the Eye by Georges Bataille (if you enjoy reading it, you're not in jeopardy of being normal)

Thus Spoke Zarathustra, A Book for All and None and *Beyond Good and Evil: Prelude to a Philosophy of the Future* by Friedrich Nietzsche

La Ronde by Arthur Schnitzler

The Dream Play and *The Ghost Sonatas* by August Strindberg

The Prince by Niccolo Machiavelli

Anything they can get their hands on by Edgar Allan Poe (They are tired of "The Raven"; too popular unless Lou Reed is doing a reading of it.)

Frankenstein by Mary Shelley

The Lulu Plays and Other Sex Tragedies by Frank Wedekind

The Marriage of Heaven and Hell by William Blake (The Doors got their name from this poem, after all.)

The Waves and *Orlando* by Virginia Woolf

Dead Souls by Nikolai Gogol

A Clockwork Orange by Anthony Burgess

Zen Must-Reads

Tao Te Ching by Lao Tsu

The Analects by Confucius

All the classical Chinese poets including Han Shan and Hồ Xuân Huởng

The Ink Dark Moon: Love Poems by Ono no Komachi and Izumi Shikibu, Women of the Ancient Court of Japan

The Book of Tea by Kakuzo Okakura

The Greening of America by Charles Reich

Rubáiyat of Omar Khayyám

Autobiography of a Yogi by Paramahansa Yogananda

Dandy Must-Reads

Confessions of an English Opium-Eater by Thomas De Quincey

Green Tea and Other Ghost Stories by J. Sheridan LeFanu

The Castle of Otranto by Horace Walpole

The Picture of Dorian Gray by Oscar Wilde

The Grammar of Ornament by Owen Jones

Poetry by Keats, Shelley, Byron, Yeats (He was in the Order of the Golden Dawn, after all.) and Samuel Taylor Coleridge (They are tolerant of Wordsworth.)

Against the Grain by J. K. Huysmans (The Dandy borrowed this from a Nouveau and never returned it.)

The Life of the Bee by Maurice Maeterlinck

Nouveau Must-Reads

Gertrude Stein, canon

Sylvia Plath, canon

Horace by George Sand (The Nouveau borrowed this from a Dandy and never returned it.)

G. E. Moore's *Principia Ethica* (a pivotal book for the Bloomsbury Group, legendary for shaping the group's values)

Savage Beauty: Biography of Edna St.Vincent Millay by Nancy Milford

The End of Alice by A. M. Homes

The Lover by Marguerite Duras

Mitsou and *Music-Hall Sidelights* by Colette

U. A. Fanthorpe, canon (The Nouveau Bohemian thinks she deserves to be the poet laureate of the U.K.)

Beat Must-Reads

A Coney Island of the Mind by Lawrence Ferlinghetti

Bomb and *Gasoline* by Gregory Corso

All the poetry of Nick Tosches

All the poetry of Charles Bukowski (Sometimes Beats just read the titles.)

Jesus' Son by Denis Johnson

Naked Lunch by William Burroughs

The Armies of the Night by Norman Mailer (It should be noted here that the Bohemian also reveres Mailer for his social consciousness and has read "The White Negro" and other essays he wrote in the late fifties and early sixties; the Bohemian adores his moxie, intellectual muscle, the sinew of his sentences. He co-founded *The Village Voice*, an alternative newspaper, and quit when it was too conservative. What's not to love?)

On the Road, The Dharma Bums et al. by Jack Kerouac

Gypsy Must-Reads

I Served the King of England by Bohumil Hrabal

Chaos, Creativity, and Cosmic Consciousness by Rupert Sheldrake, Terence McKenna, Ralph H. Abraham

Breakfast of Champions by Kurt Vonnegut

The Politics of Ecstasy by Timothy Leary, Ph.D.

A Confederate General from Big Sur and *Trout Fishing in America* by Richard Brautigan

Everything by Tom Robbins because his protagonists have included a psychedelic stockbroker, an antiwar bomber pilot and a Bohemian CIA agent

Everything by Madame Blavatsky including *Isis Unveiled* and *The Secret Doctrine*

Erotica Must-Haves

Venus in India or Love's Adventures in Hindustan by Capt. C. Deveureux (The author's mother found this racy, un-PC 1898 book in the personal effects of a dead relative and sent it to her.)

Susan Aked or Innocence Awakened, Ignorance Dispelled, published anonymously but penned by Capt. C. Deveureux

The Story of O by Pauline Réage

Delta of Venus and *Little Birds* by Anaïs Nin (Henry Miller palmed off a freelance erotica writing job to Anaïs Nin, who was happy to comply, despite the client protests of "leave out the poetry, concentrate on sex.")

Fanny Hill or Memories of a Woman of Pleasure by John Cleland

The 120 Days of Sodom by Marquis de Sade

Venus in Furs by Leopold von Sacher-Masoch

Assorted books on Tantric lovemaking (They bought these, looked at the pictures, but can't be bothered to read them.)

Bohemian Lite

The Complete Works of O. Henry

Complete Brothers Grimm Fairy Tales

A House of Pomegranates by Oscar Wilde

Alice's Adventures in Wonderland and *Through the Looking Glass* by Lewis Carroll

Goblin Market by Christina Rossetti

The Hobbit and *The Lord of the Rings* by J. R. R. Tolkien

Where the Wild Things Are by Maurice Sendak

ART

Art is a way of life to the Bohemian, so it is difficult to separate art from life. They make it. They sell it. They barter it. They inspire it. They find it on the street, on the beach, in the Dumpster, in the stars. They burn it in the fireplace when it gets too cold.

The Bohemian does not separate art from craft. Art is everything from the sculpture in the backyard made from scavenged materials to the paintings on the VW bus. Formal art training is never a requisite.

Walls, floors, shoes, shirts, sidewalks, street lamps, skylights, no surface is safe from the Bohemian with a paintbrush, marking pen or glue gun. Broken objects may become art; broken crockery or scallop shells end up as mosaics. Leftover lasagna may create a lampshade. (See Light.) It is not wise to leave a Bohemian unat-

tended in your home for any extended length of time, especially if there is alcohol or hashish around. These substances may act as a catalyst for creative ideas, which the Bohemian may generously try out on you. You could end up with a mural in the living room, find nude nymphs painted on your lampshades or your tablecloths tacked up as curtains—too much sunlight in the morning may be an irritant to the Bohemian.

If Bohemians break your mirror you may find a painting in the frame. They are sure it will be quite valuable someday.

Worst-case scenario, the Bohemian will paint all the windows black and transform the room into a camera obscura. This is usually done in a hotel.

This behavior starts early on. The student who hands in a depressed self-portrait along with a paper on existentialism (the assignment was poetry) and is sent into exile or "Independent Study" may meet the student who writes everything in Latin or French in pen and ink and wears a fox stole over her shoulder, and together, they will, in all likelihood, request a budget for painting supplies, which will be granted since they are both on the verge of genius. They will, and this is perhaps all too obvious, paint murals in the room, e.g., men in tutus with monsters growing from their armpits and strange, supernatural trees. On the back of the lampshade, underneath the public address system speaker and in other hidden places, they will paint words like *Conspiracy* and *Pervert.*

Bohemians in the making may also paint their interpretation of the story of the Middle-earth saga on their bedroom walls in the style of Aubrey Beardsley, using black markers and India ink. The parents, when finally allowed in the room after the child leaves for college or reform school, will need, to quote the mother, "five hundred coats of paint to cover it."

Bohemians like to be challenged by art; they like to be provoked, disturbed. Bohemians appreciate shock value. They will defend art condemned by the mayor and any work that outrages federally funded art organizations, even if they don't ultimately like the work.

Bohemians most admire artists who have started movements, but the wonder loses its pixie dust when the work becomes accessible or is used commercially. Bohemians used to like Magritte, for example, until his work was popularized by the advertising community.

Historically, beggars, absinthe drinkers, blind guitarists, circus folk, showgirls, prostitutes and naked people have all been acceptable and/or desirable subject matter for the Bohemian artist. Found objects disguised as art have also rattled a few nerves, for example, Duchamp's 1917 *Fountain* (a urinal), along with conceptual art that involves wrapping buildings, trees and bridges or possibly self-mutilation. Homoerotic, religiously irreverent images, phallic fantasies and barnyard vivisection[1] have also been celebrated by the Bohemian community. Bohemians champion any controversial work, as long as it reveals a poetic truth, breaks new ground or causes a scandal.

Bohemians also respect tender, personal, poetic work created by artists out of sync with the Bohemian movement of the moment. Artists cocooned, private and marginal: the romantic, homegrown surrealist Joseph Cornell, naïve un-art-museumed outsiders like Howard Finster or the ultimate outsider Henry Darger, a semi-shut-in who illustrated personal mythological worlds, psychic scrapbooks of darkly illuminated visions of young children with mix-and-match genitalia, work never meant to be viewed. And it wasn't, until he died.

1.   Artists include Robert Mapplethorpe, Andrés Serrano for his *Piss Christ,* Barney Smith and Damien Hirst.

Bohemians like to challenge, provoke and disturb. Many Bohemians think if it's not breaking a rule, inciting anarchy, igniting social reform or unsettling to the public at large, it's not good.

Bohemians commissioned to create art for public spaces refuse to compromise—will they take Lenin out of the mural at Rockefeller Center? No way, José.

CINEMA

Bohemians love films that reflect their own dereliction: manic artist, absent husband, road warrior or suicidal poet.

Subtitles do not deter the Bohemian, nor do X-rated films, unrated films, banned films, propaganda films, films eighteen hours long with no plot, and films, antique or modern, without color or sound. Films that leave the viewer devastated and sobbing in the dark are considered worthy of watching, as are documentaries on a wide range of topics from how to make chicken soup to Tourette's syndrome (this is called *Twitch and Shout,* naturally) to the films of collagist Joseph Cornell and Maya Deren. If a poet makes a film, they'll watch that, too.

Bohemians are cinematography snobs. Bohemians only see blockbusters when seriously depressed or really high, and sometimes they slum it with something by John Waters or Russ Meyers. Bohemians will see any movie that stars Klaus Kinski, Udo Kier, Conrad Veidt, Sal Mineo, James Dean, Joe Dallesandro, Max von

Sydow, Antonin Artaud, Louise Brooks, Jean Seberg, Chloë
Sevigny, Christina Ricci, Bela Lugosi, Boris Karloff, Peter Lorre,
Marlene Dietrich, Lisa Marie, Lon Chaney Senior, John Malkovich,
Richard E. Grant, Johnny Depp and Vincent Gallo.
Bohemians will watch *Cabaret* again and again
because of Joel Grey; also *Pretty Poison*
for Tuesday Weld. *Queen Christina* rates
up there with Kenneth Anger films
and *Woman in the Dunes* because even a
Bohemian is not immune to enigmatic
Greta Garbo. Expatriates of the United
Kingdom may succumb to a Hugh Grant
movie once in a while, but they will only be
reminded of why they moved from England in the first
place. The only movie in which the Bohemian has seen Tom Cruise
is Stanley Kubrick's *Eyes Wide Shut,* which made them long for
A Clockwork Orange. Bohemians are fond of saying they haven't seen
the movie, but they have read the book.

Bohemians love art films and yearn for the days when you
could smoke in the last few rows. They avoid modern complexes
and seek out fusty movie houses with mice in the aisles, moths in
the velvet curtains and kissing seats. Bohemians love Fellini nights,
Bergman marathons and features that start at midnight. Czech film
festivals are on the A-list, too, especially if they include the banned
film *Diamonds of the Night* or *Cow.* Bohemians find Bollywood an
excuse to have curry and dress up in turbans and jewels and stick a
bindi between the brows. Bohemians will go to the cinema on their
own and sprawl over two seats. They like cinemas in odd places: old
stables such as Toronto's Cinecycle and the back of bars where they
project their favorite film against brick walls for everyone to see.
Bohemians love the 16mm Bolex and Super 8s and hold Super-8

salons. They adore the experimental work of friends, particularly if they are in it.

If you ask Bohemians to name their ten favorite films they will go on and on and you will be sorry you asked. A few of these include anything by Roman Polanski, for the obvious reasons, especially *The Tenant* (every Bohemian has had a really, really bad apartment with equally bad psycho neighbors), *Knife in the Water* and *Repulsion* (they can definitely identify with killing someone who is annoying and then not having the energy to deal with the fallout), anything by Andrei Tarkovsky, Carl Theodor Dreyer, Luis Buñuel, Jean Cocteau and Federico Fellini.

Also on the list: *Eraserhead; The L-Shaped Room;* Richard Oswald's *Anders die als Andern (Different from the Others),* or rather what's left of it after the Nazis got to it—a gay pianist, a suicide; *Let's Get Lost; Vali, the Witch of Positano* (rural Utopia with a pet fox and facial tattoos); *Pull My Daisy; The Last White Shirt; Zéro de Conduite; Jules et Jim;* Tod Browning's *Freaks* (they can relate); Frank Whaley's *The Jimmy Show* (lavishly dark and defiantly un-Hollywood); *Stranger Than Paradise; Despair* (Fassbinder does Nabokov with Dirk Bogarde); *In a Year of 13 Moons* (Fassbinder again, a boy cuts it off to no avail); *Kings with Straw Mats* by poet Ira Cohen; *Buffalo 66; Gummo; Requiem for a Dream; The War Game* and *Auntie Mame* just to prove they can lighten up.

SOUND

Music is a direct feed to the emotional state of Bohemians. Music is an elixir, a magic carpet, a magic bus. It transports, soothes, excites and helps Bohemians unwind, transcend, and moves them to dance. Bohemians write their own script and lots of them make their own soundtracks. They can coax a tune from a blade of grass or make wineglasses sing. Bohemians provide live music spontaneously wherever they might be: the street, a van, an art opening, your living room. Bohemians at a dinner party are likely to break into an impromptu jam session with a strange lineup that includes an accordion, recorder and banjo. Someone may play percussion on a card table or take down the "decorative" djembe. Bohemians can wring music out of anything, from a typewriter to a balloon.

Bohemians hand out flyers to their gigs in supermarkets and on the subway. They play on the streets and rooftops and in squares and parks until they are chased away by the "authorities." Bohemians may dream about playing tribal music in Africa or sitting in for the bass player at religious snake-handling services in the deep South, but they cringe when they are invited to a karaoke night.

Bohemians will have any and every means on which to play music, vintage and state of the art. While Bohemians may resist computers, cell phones or answering machines, they will have Walkmans, Discmans or MP3 players. Bohemians still use turntables (indispensable for spinning at the new after-hours bar) and long to find a copy of *Poetry Readings in "The Cellar"* (1958), with Kenneth Rexroth reading his transgressive work to jazz grooves. Bohemians still have cassette players (including the battery-operated kind) and will purchase bootleg recordings of Anaïs Nin reading *House of Incest,* Lenny Bruce's stand-up, concerts by Patti Smith or the Grateful Dead, and there are still a few who drive around proudly in their '72 Catalina convertibles (see Wheels) blasting their eight-track cassette deck, bragging that they just picked up the soundtrack to *Shaft* at the Salvation Army for a quarter.

Bohemians with radios[2] will spend hours searching the upper and lower extremes of the AM and FM frequencies for alternative stations. If they have a shortwave radio, usually a vintage piece of furniture from the thirties or forties, they will tune in to distant stations until they find transmissions of Edith Piaf from somewhere in France to go with a night of smoking and red wine, or pick up Baaba Maal from a pirate station in Mali or South Africa.

Bohemians like to crank their music . . . literally. The appeal of the "juice-free" Victrola never wanes. Victrolas come in handy for squatters, Bohemians cut off by the electric company and Bohemians living in more primitive or "antique" dwellings, not to

---

2.   Radios are also a source for alternative news. Bohemians do not trust the networks or the mainstream press. They will choose the BBC over CNN and Pacifica Radio over both.

mention California Bohemians affected by rolling blackouts. Bohemians search out old 78s of Xavier Cugat or folk music from the Ukraine or assorted 1920s fox-trots.

The Bohemian's taste in music is expansive and could be a book unto itself. Bohemians listen to Bach's preludes and fugues for organ, Nico and The Velvet Underground, Aorta, Astor Piazzolla's tangos, Japanese koto music, Belle & Sebastian, Goldfrapp, Ibrahim Ferrer, Om Kalsoum, Dizzy Gillespie and Björk. Simply put, the Bohemian is as comfortable listening to a song by Radiohead as to a Shostakovich string quartet.

Bohemians are constantly on the lookout for something new. Listening to NPR while driving late one night, they might hear cellist Arthur Russell singing "Losing My Taste for the Night Life." Eerie and hypnotic, they will find it the perfect soundtrack for the night road, their "lost highway." They will, of course, buy the CD.

Bohemians love art bands, especially if they are raw and rough. They embrace musicians and groups until they are swept up by the American mainstream—that's when Bohemians lose all respect. Bohemians are fond of saying, "I used to like so-and-so until they went commercial." They still adore Laurie Anderson even though their yuppie brother went to see her.

Bohemians follow world music, important since so much music in America and Europe has become a corporate product. Bohemians seek out grassroots musicianship from Ghana, Senegal, Cuba and Uruguay and music created in places where chickens are still allowed on the bus. However, world music that corrupts the rhythm of indigenous music and replaces it with a western disco beat is not highly favored. Bohemian favorites include Salif Keita, Baaba Maal, Paco De Lucía, Tomatito, Cesaria Evora, Caetano Veloso, Susana Baca, Maria Bethânia, Zakir Hussain, Ismael Lo, Fela Kuti, Dimi Mint Abba and Cheikha Rimitti, to name a few.

When it comes to jazz, Bohemians are discriminating, opinionated and contradictory. The Bohemian's first choice is not traditional jazz like Louis Armstrong and Benny Goodman, though they may be represented on several 78s sandwiched between a Scott Joplin cakewalk and rag. Bohemians prefer adventuresome modernists like Ornette Coleman. Glenn Miller is tricky: "In the Mood" puts some Bohemians out of the mood, but they swoon to "Pagan Love Song."

Bohemians, Beats in particular, will stay up until sunrise polishing off a bottle of ouzo while debating the greatest trumpeters, bassists and pianists. They wax about the sax and the variety of sounds that virtuosos blow from it, e.g., Stan Getz, Charlie Parker, Zoot Sims, Paul Desmond and Dexter Gordon.

Bohemian jazz connoisseurs worship Miles Davis almost on the level of God. The Bohemian's spiritual guide is most likely John Coltrane, though some argue it's Alice Coltrane. Bohemians respect Pharaoh Sanders' psychedelic sax slurs. Their favorite Sanders album is *Thembi,* which assists them with "astral traveling."

At present, the Bohemian listens to Cassandra Wilson, Mahavishnu Orchestra, Charlie Hunter, Pat Martino, Wayne Shorter and Joe Zawinul, and of course, Bohemians have always loved Charles Mingus, Jack Teagarden, Chet Baker and Thelonious Monk—Bohemians wish they could have heard him jam at a Harlem rent party.

Bohemians enjoy all classical music and are open to everything from Mozart to Mahler to John Cage. They appreciate Cage's silent piece, "4' 33" " as much as Morton Subotnik's seminal composition "Silver Apples of the Moon." Bohemians are heartbroken that *Eine Kleine Nachtmusik* has been abused by television and radio advertising.

When there is hot water, the Bohemian likes to take a bath—sea salt, epsom salt or their favorite oil, e.g., lavender or patchouli, while listening to string quartets by Béla Bartók or "Claire de Lune" by Debussy. Beethoven is considered to be on the same plane as Miles Davis, especially Symphony No. 9 and the second movement of Symphony No. 7. Perhaps the favorite piece of the Bohemian is *The Rite of Spring* by Stravinsky or *Finlandia* by Sibelius. Saint-Saëns' *Danse Macabre* and Schubert's *Death and the Maiden* are also irresistible.

Zen Bohemians might listen to the songs of the humpback whales but are not fans of Yanni or Kenny G. Zens listen to real meditative music: Ali Akbar Khan, Nusrat Fateh Ali Khan, all northern Indian music played according to the proper time of day as dictated by the particular raga. Gamelan music and Balinese monkey chant also work. The Beats' favorite vocalist may be Billie Holiday, though Tom Waits runs a close second with his seedy, down-and-out lyrics. They consider him a poet, along with Nick Cave. The Fairy Folk Bohemian will listen to lute music, dulcimer, Gregorian chant and harp music. The Gypsy Bohemian adores the balalaika, the bouzouki and calliope music, and at the risk of being predictable, they like the Gipsy Kings and *Carmina Burana*. Given the chance the Gypsy will choose medieval music from Andalusia, a mélange of Jewish, Christian and Muslim rhythms. Gypsies of the Hippie persuasion are into Dylan, Joan Baez, Janis Joplin, Country Joe and the Fish. They love music from the psychedelic era: The Beatles' *Sgt. Pepper's Lonely Hearts Club Band,* Jimi Hendrix, The Doors, Jefferson Airplane's *Surrealistic Pillow* and Germany's experimental acid group Can. The Dandy listens to the glass harmonica or eighteenth-century opera while grooming and dressing (the Dandy loves all the cross-dressing in Mozart's *Le Nozze di Figaro*) and then moves on to early Bowie or T. Rex. André Claveau's *Fumée* is perfect for a sunset. The Dandy will serve a midnight glass of Chartreuse while listening to Clara Rockmore on the theremin.

Do Not Write in This Space

V
NINE BOHEMIAN CASE STUDIES

NINE BOHEMIAN
CASE STUDIES

STARRING the ABSINTHE-SIPPING
BELLY DANCER OONA, DANTINI the
MAGNIFICENT, the ANGEL BOY and OTHER
MODERN-DAY BOHEMIANS

Percy, painter/musician

Oona, actress

Heathcoate, portrait painter/muralist/navigator

Cody, sculptor

Dantini, magician

Ishimoto, journalist/angel

Ryan, yoga instructor/general labor foreman

Atlas, painter/writer/musician

Zouzou, photographer/painter/photo gallery curator

Percy

Painter/musician

AGE:	24
ASTROLOGICAL SIGN:	Pisces
BORN:	Wicklow, Ireland
CURRENT DWELLING:	the basement of an off-off Broadway theater in Manhattan
FAVORITE BOOKS:	*Ulysses* by James Joyce; *The Adventures of Sherlock Holmes* by Sir Arthur Conan Doyle
FAVORITE MUSIC:	Astor Piazzolla; eighteenth-century harp music; The Pogues
FAVORITE MOVIES:	*Withnail and I; The Hound of the Baskervilles* with Basil Rathbone
FAVORITE FOODS:	scones with clotted cream and orange marmalade; fish-and-chips
FAVORITE DRINKS:	Port; Guinness
MOTTO:	Pursue happiness at no expense.

Eighteen months in Paris sketching tourists in Pigalle was enough; Percy wanted to sample Bohemian life, American style. There was his art teacher in Dublin with an aunt on Fifth Avenue across from the park who needed her spaniels walked while she wintered in Spain until she returned for the Westminster Dog Show. That was enough to get Percy on a plane—standby, sleeping two nights at the airport—guitar, paints, brushes and a suitcase full of snazzy,

PERCY'S WARDROBE

one burgundy velvet shirt

two tailored violet shirts

three ruffled violet shirts

linen poet's shirt

tweed jacket, three buttons

Levi's 501 jeans, indigo, two pairs

Levi's 505 jeans, black, one pair

baggy black pants a little on the short side

black wool turtleneck

black wool V-neck sweater

black vintage cardigan of unknown fibers, possibly cashmere; holes in elbows

tweed overcoat

fedora

black velvet beret

smoking jackets in burgundy, ultramarine and black

rumpled, Basil Rathbone meets Oscar Wilde threads.

The building was swank, with a decked-out doorman and marble lobby. And the apartment was bigger than his grandmother's cottage in Wicklow, larger even than his parents' house. A wrap-around terrace facing Central Park, Oriental and Aubusson carpets, Chinese black and red lacquered furniture mingled with some important Empire pieces. Four bedrooms and the softest sheets he'd ever felt. He was happy to find twelve different types of tea in the cupboard and enough food in the refrigerator and on the shelves to last a month. He had eighty-seven dollars in his wallet, which was, by the way, worn thin. There was a stipend taped to the refrigerator for tips and miscellaneous expenses totaling three hundred dollars in cash and he figures that's enough to live on for a few months, unless, of course, he hits the pubs, which is likely. He was delighted to find washing machines in the building and, with a small box of dye from the pharmacy, dyed his shirts violet when the coffee and wine stains got the upper hand.

For weeks he painted portraits of people, mostly girls, he met in the park, sometimes bringing the girls back. He saw an ad in *The Village Voice* and joined a band.

Played two gigs at CBGB's. Things were going pretty well until he tried selling his paintings in front of the building. He was skeptical now about "inalienable rights." And what about red, white and blue freedom? What of *his* pursuit of happiness? Hadn't New Yorkers seen nudes before? He takes his work across the street and sets up not far from the art museum. The tourists seem to love him. Girls in particular take to the show-quality spaniels, which he takes with him for just this reason.

December has barely started when the telegram comes from Spain giving him two days to move out. Why did they bother to make the building's washing machines public, available to all, and for a price, too, if there were restrictions such as the forbidding of dyeing shirts violet? How could he have known Mrs. Lambeth's towels and undies would turn lavender, along with her husband's shirts? To Percy it was clearly an improvement. And it wasn't as if he had the band rehearsing at three in the morning. Ten o'clock could scarcely be called the shank of the evening. He was more than considerate, he always stopped well before midnight.

Fortunately, the doorman, Anthony, has dreamed of acting ever since seeing *The Sopranos*—"It don't look too hard, I could do that"—and has been on auditions at a theater downtown. Voilá. The ad he gave Percy read: "Living arrangements available in exchange for set painting and construction."

Percy's current scenario:

A Midsummer-Night's Dream forest in painted wood from last year's production creates the entrance to his "space," the walk-in wardrobe closet in the basement of the theater lighted with an ornate chandelier of clear and amethyst cut-glass. His canvases lean up against fairy-tale trees, and his bed, a satin-covered chaise longue, is an old prop. His clothing hangs on a rolling rack burgeoning with theatrical costumes, most of which he finds appropriate for private and public use. From Shakespearean doublets and lace-cuffed shirts to Noël Coward smoking jackets, nothing is too Dandy for the debonair Dubliner; and there's plenty on the rack for his models. He asks them to slip into Pre-Raphaelite robes, kimonos and showgirl stars and spangles before moving on to sketching them nude.

Part of the deal for living there requires him to read lines now and then, and today he is standing in for Laertes, reading for all five of the Ophelia callbacks. In his mind he, too, is holding auditions, for models, muses and lovers.

Oona

Actress

AGE:	27
ASTROLOGICAL SIGN:	Sagittarius
BORN:	birth certificate states Sweden
CURRENT DWELLING:	New York
FAVORITE BOOKS:	*The Hunchback of Notre-Dame* by Victor Hugo; *The Gift* by Hafiz of Shiraz; *The Soul of Rumi: A New Collection of Ecstatic Poems; My Double Life, The Memoirs of Sarah Bernhardt*
FAVORITE MUSIC:	Yma Sumac; Björk; whirling dervish music
FAVORITE MOVIE:	*The Passion of Joan of Arc* by Carl Theodor Dreyer
FAVORITE FOODS:	beluga caviar, Kumamoto oysters; Coney Island hot dogs
FAVORITE DRINKS:	Champagne and absinthe
MOTTO:	Why not?

Oona is tall, Swedish and, unbeknownst to her Bohemian friends, a princess. All her actor and artist friends live in squalid Lower East Side, Brooklyn or Harlem apartments. Flickering lights in hallways, mattresses on the floor, candles in wine bottles, crooked stairs. She was jealous!

OONA'S WARDROBE

*Despite her Bohemian
longings, there is not
enough room in this book
to outline all of Oona's
closet. Her social obliga-
tions require her to have
ballgowns and cocktail
dresses, and since it is
not fashionable to be
seen repetitively in the
same outfit in high
society, she has, at this
writing, thirty-two
cocktail dresses, twenty-
seven gowns, fifteen of
them couture, and two
custom-made tuxedos.
(Designers range from
Oscar de la Renta—he
was good enough for
Jackie O—and Geoffrey
Beene to Zac Posen and
John Galliano.) Even
this is a modest sum for
a princess, and the
numbers are in constant
flux. This is because
there are rules. Anything
worn more than five
times, unless it is an
extremely simple
silhouette, she donates to
Housing Works. Anything
in which she has been
photographed, for
fashion trades or
magazines, she donates
immediately. She does
not consider herself
frivolous, spoiled or
wasteful. These are, in
essence, her work clothes.
She is more comfortable
in her vintage clothing,
denim jeans and skirts,*

After her peace mission to Israel with the Sufis last year—she is determined to make a documentary of their next one—she knew she could no longer bend to her mother's will. She'd had enough of her family's Upper East Side six-bedroom apartment with Persian carpets and slate-blue walls, furniture that had been in the family for centuries and large oil paintings of horses and ancestors; she'd let her brother have it.

She was looking for something earth-ier, downtown, something Bohemian. Her artist lover, Heathcoate Douglas Wyndham, suggested the Bowery when she said she was looking for a place to buy.

It seemed impossible to find Bohemia uptown—Sotheby's, Christie's, overpriced antique shops and designer shoe salons, hotel bars that charge twenty-one dollars for a glass of mediocre Champagne. She felt uncomfortable making love uptown in a spacious and deluxe apartment, her every kiss overseen by the overbearing ancestors who disapproved (she could see it in their grey painted eyes and in the straight stern expression of their thin lips) of the Bohemian boyfriend who had never had a job or filed taxes. It seemed impos-sible to be taken seriously as a struggling actress with a blue-blood address. Oona dismissed the maid and the cook when she moved downtown not far from the Jean Cocteau Theatre and the famous, seedy music club CBGB's. In true Bohemian spirit, Oona chose the top floor, the fifth, for her Bowery loft. Heathcoate admonished her for the bourgeois convenience of an elevator but he has yet to take the stairs.

She's starting life anew as a Bohemian, a cosmopolitan actress devoted to the arts, looking to be enriched by her new environment, to create her own internal environment, to escape the social system to which she'd become accustomed and enslaved. She will cook, clean, act, suffer. She's already getting publicity for suffering. At Easter she sat vigil for forty-eight hours as Mary Magdalene in the basement of a local theater for its annual fund-raiser.

She hosts catered dinner parties at her new space, orders contraband absinthe and cases of Nicolas Feuillatte Champagne— she met the owner of the Champagne company at a party and loved that he has homes on four continents; he told her that his Champagne is for "the bourgeois bohème or bourgeois people who became Bohemians in their way of life, but still can't get rid of their education." She decided instantly that it was her favorite.

in cotton shirts from India, in kimonos, in nothing.

Of course there are dozens of maillots and bikinis, T-shirts, gauzy bits of fabric and belly dancing costumes. Lingerie? She is a minimalist.

Shoes. That is another story. Whenever possible she is barefoot—her mother blames the Gypsies in Czechoslovakia where Oona was born a month early—but for occasions requiring footwear she can choose from her sixteen pairs of espadrilles, water buffalo sandals, sandals embellished with turquoise and coral and shells, ninety-six pairs in all, and all designer names. Names, names, names. It's her belief in them that distresses her. If she were a true Bohemian she would have nothing but disdain for labels. She wants to shed herself of them. To exist without them, to believe in herself. She doesn't need their names to validate her. She will overcome.

She demands that everyone change seats between courses; she asks the newly published authors to autograph their books, of which she has purchased dozens. Cocktail parties are also an excuse for the unveiling of a new painting she's purchased at a friend's opening. Another friend will be there to sing an aria for the occasion.

The bed, which is normally in plain view, is given a modicum of privacy with a folding screen on which Heathcoate has painted a reclining nude of Oona as a goddess. She wonders if goddesses have insomnia, because she has it frequently. She views "troubled sleep" as a Bohemian virtue. This is when she reads disturbing poetry by Antonin Artaud in its original French, works on her monologue from Oscar Wilde's *Salomé,* or throws something on and drinks cheap red wine from an unbreakable cup across the street at CBGB's.

Oona, now that it's warmer, comes to Heathcoate's unheated studio, a room right below his apartment in the West Village, and sits for another nude portrait.

She loves him for stirring her out of complacency, for making her feel like a Venus or an actress. Even from across the room the paint under his nails is evident. Oona doesn't mind the paint. *Au contraire.* She longs for Heathcoate to stroke her neck with his viridian-green-stained fingers, streak vermilion over her collarbone, cobalt blue between her toes.

Paint is warm, intoxicating, vital, dirty and playful.

Just last night he invited her to belly dance on board his friend's restored lightship for its nightclub debut. Two artists said they would like to paint her, and a poet scribbled an impromptu verse about her on a cocktail napkin and read it over the ship's loudspeaker. Oona is beginning to realize that being a muse might be a full-time job.

Heathcoate

Portrait painter/muralist/navigator

AGE:	37
ASTROLOGICAL SIGN:	Cancer
BORN:	Pennsylvania
CURRENT DWELLINGS:	West Village studio and a lightship
FAVORITE BOOKS:	*Moby-Dick* by Herman Melville; the Aubrey/Maturin series by Patrick O'Brian; *20,000 Leagues Under the Sea* by Jules Verne; currently rereading his childhood favorite, the Horatio Hornblower series by C. S. Forester
FAVORITE MUSIC:	Antonio Vivaldi's *The Four Seasons;* Grandmaster Flash and the Furious Five
FAVORITE MOVIES:	*Ruggles of Red Gap* with Charles Laughton; *Mutiny on the Bounty* with Charles Laughton; *The Man Who Would Be King*
FAVORITE FOODS:	cherry pie with vanilla ice cream; Chinese takeout
FAVORITE DRINK:	gin
MOTTO:	Something by Juan Ramón Jiménez he read in a science fiction journal: If they give you ruled paper, write the other way.

HEATHCOATE'S WARDROBE

five white shirts, frayed cuffs

tuxedo pants

one pair tails

black dinner jacket

grey kidskin gloves

black watch cap

Greek fisherman's cap

grey wide-brim fedora with black band, vintage, purchased at the WWII reenactment and airshow in Reading, Pennsylvania

navy wool sweater, holes in elbows, assorted moth holes

Aran Islands knit sweater from flea market

black gloves, fingers cut off

Austrian cape

long navy coat with brass buttons

black jeans, two pairs, one of them paint-streaked

black engineer boots

farm boots

canvas Chinese slippers from Chinatown

Wellingtons

Heathcoate's friends call him Captain Nemo and sometimes Lord Byron. Even the newish clothing he picks up at thrift shops or at army-navy stores takes on the look of a more distant time once he's done with it. With navy-issue wool sweaters, he wears a Greek fisherman's cap and a long navy coat with brass buttons. He always turns up the collars of his white shirts and ties an ascot or narrow silk scarf around his neck and removes the buttons from his cuffs so he can punch through cuff links, many of which he's fashioned himself from military insignias, medals and scrimshaw. He uses a quill pen, writes his journal on the unused pages of a ship's log from the 1890s and has never owned a television. Years ago, with too much idle time on a snowy night, he gave himself a small tattoo of an anchor between his thumb and fore-finger.

Heathcoate's best friend, the curator of a nautical museum, bought a run-down lightship called *The Frying Pan,* which he docks at Pier 63 at 23rd Street. Heathcoate lives on it most of the summer. They plan to turn it into a nightclub.

Otherwise, Heathcoate lives in Greenwich Village in a single room with a sink, loft bed and veranda large enough for two wrought-iron chairs and a tiny table, all of which show signs of rust. A little flea-market taxidermy here and there: a fruit bat hanging from the ceiling, a barn owl on a branch, twin baby deer with wire showing through the legs and two baby chicks struggling over a rubber worm. Next to his antique sextant, and nestled in between his daguerreotype collection, an animal fetus of some sort floats in a jar of cloudy formaldehyde. People are always asking him what kind of a fetus it is. It's an aardvark, he'll say, or a monkey. He never says the same animal twice.

The toilet and shower are one floor down, shared by other residents and the homeless people who wander into the building because the lock on the front door is broken. He brings his own lightbulb unless he doesn't have one, then he brings the flashlight. When the battery's dead he uses a candle. He brings his own toilet paper, too. When he's out of that, *The Yellow Pages*.

When Heathcoate brings girls home they tell him his apartment is very interesting, but they hardly ever come back. Until Oona, his new lover, who confessed to him that she was a Swedish princess but only after their second bottle of Champagne.

Heathcoate appropriated the apartment beneath his when it became vacant due to the tenant's overdose; now it's his art studio. He wears a 1930s tuxedo while painting.

Oona buys him nineteenth-century crystal glasses and thinks it's charming that he uses them to hold paintbrushes and pencils.

He loves her for making his life seem more romantic. He should feel shabby next to her, but she makes him feel authentic, like a genuine artist, as though everything about him were precious—his threadbare jacket and fraying shirt cuffs, the paint under his nails, his pathos, his poverty. She even delights in sharing dinners with him in his studio—macaroni and cheese or ramen noodles cooked on a hot plate. He is seduced, too, by her spontaneity, her impromptu ticket purchases to Bermuda, Marrakech, Rome. His previous girlfriend bought him a nailbrush.

Heathcoate's latest show is in the East Village, but he will not sell three of his pieces: a particularly haunting and rather lumpy oil of his dead grandfather, which includes his cremains blended in with the paint; one of Charlemagne, his white cat, which features tufts of the dead animal's fur; and a plaster cast of his dead ferret. There will be, just for the record, no inquiries on these particular works.

The rest of the show—largely nocturnal seascapes—sells out, and for the first time in years, Heathcoate has pocket money. He takes his friends to dinner at Balthazar, and over bottles of Champagne and towers of oysters, mussels and crab claws, they decide to sail the lightship to Baltimore. He's been commissioned to paint several murals for the new Madame Tussaud's wax museum. He hopes they pay him in cash; he has never paid taxes.

Cody

Sculptor

AGE:	30
ASTROLOGICAL SIGN:	Leo
BORN:	Baltimore, Maryland
CURRENT DWELLING:	Baltimore
FAVORITE BOOKS:	*Gray's Anatomy of the Human Body; The Autobiography of Benvenuto Cellini;* working his way through the following authors: George Eliot, Edith Wharton, Anthony Trollope, Nathaniel Hawthorne
FAVORITE MUSIC:	Jack Teagarden; Donizetti; Puccini. *Madama Butterfly* never fails to make him cry.
FAVORITE MOVIE:	*La Dolce Vita*
FAVORITE FOODS:	*moules et frittes;* "Marco Polo" cuisine
FAVORITE DRINK:	springwater. "You cut out the flavors and get down to the essence when you operate on a shoestring."
MOTTO:	Don't call me before noon, man.

Cody is slightly larger than life. Not just because he is gregariously flamboyant but because he is built on a larger scale than most humans. He is six feet four inches, has large hands, large eyes and a large head. Cody is a sculptor, and most of his work is larger than

CODY'S WARDROBE

*twenty-five hats,
including*

> *two ivory linen caps*
>
> *two black Basque
> berets*
>
> *plaid driver's cap*
>
> *porkpie*
>
> *stingy brim*
>
> *watch cap*
>
> *prayer cap*
>
> *batik hat from
> Mozambique*
>
> *African print hat*
>
> *army-navy hat with
> earflaps and fleece
> lining*

*four white shirts with
no sleeves*

*two white shirts
with sleeves sporting
monograms, not his own*

two black turtlenecks

*French sailor's shirt,
navy and white stripes*

*three white
sleeveless undershirts
(vernacular—
wife beaters)*

two plaid shirts

*navy sweatshirt worn
inside out*

*navy sweatshirt worn
inside out with sleeves
cut off*

*two V-neck wool sweaters,
one navy and one red,
conspicuous moth holes*

life-size, too: colossal breasts and der-rières carved in wood. Large feet carved in wood. Large heads sculpted in clay. He has just finished the head of Albert Einstein and is working on a six-foot clay sculpture of Saint Teresa in ecstasy. A young ballerina is modeling.

Cody started out on Reade Street in Baltimore where he and Pete, a poet, philosopher of life, lover of women and screenwriter, shared an apartment. When he got a gallery in Baltimore he traded up. Moved to Fell's Point and rented a small house in an alley, where fetid water laps the concrete banks, the air stinks of damp and the cobblestones are always wet.

A former servant's house, it is small but has three floors. His studio is on the top floor. He found his chairs on the street. The caning was shot so he stretched bicycle inner tubes to form seats and backs. Knowing his proclivity for innovative repair, antique shops unload treasures of unimagined beauty in various states of disrepair in front of his house: a table with three legs, the above-mentioned unuphol-stered chairs, broken chandeliers, antique mannequins. He particularly likes the mannequins. They are well-mannered and stylish companions, and he has engaged them in various activities around the house, dressed and undressed; they are having conversations and cocktails, and one is doing a little nude modeling for the mannequin artist with a pencil and sketch pad.

Cody likes to cook and invented what he calls "Marco Polo" cuisine. He combines traditional Chinese and Italian ingredients, like red sauce over Chinese noodles, grated Parmesan over fried rice. His specialty is Peking lasagna. It is because of this that the lampshades all cast a romantic amber-colored light. He once overestimated the amount of lasagna he'd need for a dinner party and stretched the leftover noodles, still wet, over wire hangers he'd bent into a lampshade frame. When he saw how good it looked, he made more. Cody is infinitely resourceful. His washing machine is an industrial plastic bucket with a plunger. His toilet paper dispenser is the outstretched arm of a bronze Roman warrior.

Cody shaves in the kitchen. He uses a straight razor that hangs over the sink near the espresso pot. He shaves only the sides, then trims his goatee.

Cody is represented by a gallery in New York on 57th Street and is waiting for his second solo show. New York, he declares, is the capital of capitalism; it provides a sort of entertainment, a theater of conformism. He is contemplating taking

wool fisherman's sweater, tightly woven, in navy

navy peacoat

two pairs sandals: one water buffalo, the other black rubber from Chinatown in New York

desert boots

black wingtips

flip-flops in brown

sneakers with toe portion cut off, perforated for ventilation the fourth-floor walk-up a friend found for him in Chinatown; it's large, well lighted and, being on the top floor on the fringe of Manhattan, cheap. He will stay true to his ideals in this theater of conformism. Besides, he knows clowns, sword fighters and mimes in New York; it's bound to be amusing.

He is reading about the life and work of Michelangelo. Cody has great respect for the last, "unfinished" sculptures of Michelangelo, figures emerging from choppy rough stone. They are finished, he has decided. Michelangelo was embracing the nature of the materials, the power, the machismo of stone. He leaves his book on Michelangelo on the coffee table, which is made of an amoeba-shaped piece of glass that he has cut himself and rested on wrought-iron legs.

Girls like having an art book to peruse while he makes them coffee or hunts for last night's wine bottle. When said girl gets to the unfinished sculptures he tells the girl his theory. He declares that artists alone have the right to interpret art, the intentions of dead artists, that artists alone have an edge.

Usually the girl is an art student at the Maryland Institute or a nude model at the Maryland Institute, but sometimes the girl is a poet or a dance student. The girl is always impressed and ends up on the futon.

When Cody sells a piece of sculpture to a private collector in New York, he takes Pete to Bertha's Mussels for dinner. He brings a date, a mannequin dressed in a tattered evening gown, sequins dangling by threads. At this point, he's gone through just about all the real girls in Baltimore. Moving to New York might not be a bad idea.

Dantini the Magnificent

Magician

AGE:	70-something
ASTROLOGICAL SIGN:	Aries
BORN:	Prague, Romania or possibly Poland, the story changes
CURRENT DWELLING:	Baltimore
FAVORITE BOOKS:	*Houdini on Magic* by Harry Houdini; *Trilby* by George du Maurier
FAVORITE MUSIC:	*Firebird Suite* by Stravinsky
FAVORITE MOVIES:	*Destiny* by Fritz Lang; *The Overcoat* by Alexei Batalov
FAVORITE FOODS:	figs; Vienna sausages
FAVORITE DRINK:	Turkish coffee
MOTTO:	Now you see it, now you don't. Life is but a dream.

Dantini the Magnificent does magic at the Peabody Bookstore downtown on Friday nights. He is polished but vintage; you can see how the trick with the silver magic rings is done, as if it is in slow motion. He wears a turban, black with gold beads, for this bookstore magic show. On special occasions he wears the red turban with gold dragons. Otherwise he wears a hat like Frank Sinatra's.

His eyes are wildly blue like a hyacinth and his hair, peppered and coarsely salted to a tarnished silver. There are small pillows

DANTINI'S WARDROBE

fez

Turkish slippers

Moroccan slippers

two pairs black wingtips

black Keds

tweed jacket, elbows worn

tweed overcoat with burgundy silk lining, slightly shredded

black velvet cape with gold clasp

tuxedo pants

assorted trousers in dark, nondescript colors

five French-cuff white shirts, heavily starched, with mother-of-pearl buttons

cuff links, including a pair of crystal balls, and the Egyptian god Anubis in obsidian

six vests, assorted silks and wools

assorted silk scarves and ascots in paisley, polka dots, Parisian monument motifs and solids

silk monogrammed pajamas, five pairs, only one bearing his own monogram, which was entirely by coincidence

three turbans

top hat, also used as a prop

two fedoras

beneath his eyes, and his long beard shows no evidence of grooming.

His shirts are white, always, and crisply starched but greying and frayed at the collar and cuffs. A herringbone tweed jacket, his favorite day wear, is paired with dark pants and white Converse sneakers. In good weather and on special occasions he wears Turkish slippers.

Dantini lives in a second floor walk-up. Crooked stairs, a German Expressionist hallway with no right angles. A bell tinkles when the door is opened, and you enter a room in splendid ruins, part old-world hotel lobby, part Gypsy caravan, part occult museum.

Magical accoutrements everywhere: crystal balls, black silk top hats, large silver rings, scarves, boxes with secret compartments. On the walls, antique magic show posters; one of Medusa, the snake charmer. On the marble fireplace mantel are photos of Houdini and other magicians and a porcelain phrenology bust.

There is an antique birdcage for the dove, metal and painted green, hanging near one of the windows. There is dust everywhere.

A nineteenth-century Italian couch with stout, ornate, carved legs is badly in need of reupholstery but is proud in its threadbareness, the brocade fabric coming off the back brazen in its display of the inner workings, the construction of the couch, as if it, too, will reveal how the magic is done.

On the table, a thin Turkish carpet and china set out as if a tea party is about to happen, and one is. First, there is Mimi, the filmmaker from Barcelona with the red-wine voice. She'll be filming his magic show this evening and documenting his life for a few weeks. And then there is the beautiful woman he saw in Fell's Point on his way home last night as she was fluttering into Bertha's Mussels. He consulted the cards and they told him he'd see her again. That she'd play a significant part in his future. He imagines her in a glittering pink dress, perfect for levitating and disappearing acts. He still has this dress in a trunk.

The china was his grandmother's, one of the few things that remain. It is from Czechoslovakia and is pink and white. He wonders if the fluttering woman would rather have Champagne than tea.

Sitting at its own little desk near the table is a glassy-eyed young blond, an eighteenth-century automaton that can write and draw a horse.

eye patch

cigarette holder

white gloves

There are peacock feathers in a tall slender silver vase. In another vase, Czechoslovakian hand-painted porcelain, black roses more than twenty years old. Dantini packs his magic top hat, rings, scarves, cards, floating ball, dove and other supplies. Tonight he'll wear the red turban with gold dragons. Red is his lucky color.

When he gets to the Peabody Bookstore, Dantini is nervous. He has not been nervous in years. He is not nervous because of Mimi and her small crew, who have set up a camera with a bright floodlight in the corner. Mimi is testing a boom mike when he comes in. She has long, wispy braids. Dense, dark eyebrows with only a little thinning to separate them. Red lipstick, the kind of red you can see across a room. Across the street. Across a river. Six earrings in her right ear. Wristlets with dangles and bangles. Necklaces streaming into cleavage. They tinkle. "Testing, testing," she is saying with her red lips, and then she sees him. He is nervous because the cards tell him something unexpected will happen.

He stands in the shadows searching the small crowd to find his assistant for the evening. Voilà. The gauzy, fluttering woman he saw in Fell's Point enters. He will make her disappear.

The bookshop owner comes out from behind the bar, wipes her hands on her apron.

"Ladies and gentlemen, welcome to the magic show at the Peabody Bookstore. I'm very pleased to present to you a conjurer extraordinaire—Dantini the Magnificent. Dantini has traveled the world, gathering mystic strength from the earth's power centers, Mount Athos and Delphi in Greece, the pyramids in Egypt, Hebron, Chartres Cathedral and Stonehenge. He's mystified sultans, monarchs and emperors. He's given tips to Ricky Jay and sipped absinthe with Blackstone.

"Let's give a warm welcome to Dantini the Magnificent!"

The gold dragons of his turban flicker under the lamp where

he does the trick with large silvery rings. The rings shimmer. He moves them slowly, too slowly. And then he brings out the cards. He asks the gauzy woman to pick a card, any card, and notices she has ordered red wine, she drinks wine, but of course she does, there is no Champagne here at the bookstore café. She looks too refined to be here, like a princess. And there is something mysterious in her eyes.

She picks the queen of diamonds.

He guesses and she claps. Everyone claps. Another round. She picks another card.

The king of diamonds. What are the odds of this, he thinks, it's kismet, fate, it's truly in the cards. In the old days he had a stage and a girl to saw in half and a dozen doves. Now he is down to one dove and no girl. He wants to see her in a shimmering showgirl ensemble. "It would be a pleasure to saw you in two," he says to the gauzy woman. Everyone laughs.

He does the number with the floating ball, then the dove. It flies from a scarf. The dove circles the room, then lights on the outstretched hand of the gauzy woman. She stands and gyrates a little, then swirls dervishly. The dove stays. The cameraman catches everything.

Dantini claps and holds out his top hat. The dove returns to him, lands on the brim of the hat, then steps inside. He taps the bottom of the hat with his wand and it collapses. The dove is gone! Everyone applauds. Dantini bows. A few more scarf tricks, then the grand finale.

"I need a volunteer," he says. "Who would like to disappear?"

Several women raise their hands. He chooses the gauzy woman.

"Have we ever done this before?" he asks her.

"No," she says, "we have never done this before."

He opens a large sarcophagus for her to step into; the dove flies out. Everyone gasps. Even Mimi the filmmaker. The gauzy woman steps in and lies down and Dantini closes the lid. He covers it with shiny black fabric. He says an incantation in a language no one understands. He waves a wand, there is an explosion of bright light, a wizard's poof, blue smoke, lots of it. He whips off the cloth, and when he opens the box, the girl is gone. The crowd gasps again.

Dantini bows. "Good night, my friends. Thank you for coming."

Someone yells, "Where's the lady?"

Dantini shrugs. "She'll come back when she wants to."

The bookstore door creaks open. The gauzy woman steps inside. She looks mystified.

Everyone applauds, and Dantini bows again. He gathers his things, puts them in a black case, the dove in a small box, then joins Mimi and her crew at a table. The waiter brings him a bottle of water and a Turkish coffee.

The gauzy woman snuggles up to him. "I love your dove."

Dantini raises an eyebrow. Takes a sip of coffee. "Would you like to be levitated someday?"

Mimi whispers to her, "Are you part of the act?"

She winks at Dantini. "I'm his new assistant!"

Mimi continues filming as Dantini has a coffee with his "assistant." His teeth are the color of sparrows. She follows him and the girl to his apartment, films him pouring tea, taking off his turban, putting away the dove, the floating ball, the rings. The girl sits next to the automaton. "You have a doll?"

"Her name is Lucritia," says Dantini. He winds her up. She dips a quill pen into an inkwell and writes "Oona."

"That's my name," cries the gauzy woman. "How did you do that?"

Lucritia dips her quill into the ink and draws a horse.

Ishimoto

Journalist/angel

AGE:	33
ASTROLOGICAL SIGN:	Aquarius
BORN:	Kyoto, Japan
CURRENT DWELLING:	Rochambeau Hotel, Baltimore
FAVORITE BOOKS:	*The Decay of an Angel* by Yukio Mishima; *A House of Pomegranates* by Oscar Wilde
FAVORITE MUSIC:	*Merry Christmas, Mr. Lawrence* by Ryuichi Sakamoto
FAVORITE MOVIES:	*It's a Wonderful Life; Wings of Desire*
FAVORITE FOODS:	angel food cake; cotton candy; gummy bears
FAVORITE DRINK:	rare white tea
MOTTO:	People are so much kinder when you have wings.

By the age of seven, Ishimoto was famous for his flower arrangements which explored the fundamental theories of Tokugawa decoration. He wrote poetry and painted watercolors of monkeys, mushrooms, mermaids, fairies and fish. He was too shy to give presentations in front of the class and was not good at sports. Despite these shortcomings, Ishimoto was popular. By twelve he was giving puppet shows. Even adults came to see them. He wrote all the scripts and constructed all the costumes from sequins, satin and shiny paper.

Ishimoto had always been fond of shimmering surfaces. He painted his fingernails with nacreous glazes, collected pearls, shells and nineteenth- and early twentieth-century lusterware and considered oceanography as a career until it occurred to him that deep sea diving, with its unappealing zip-on outfit, was part of the picture. He attended the Sorbonne and studied literature, journalism and the arts and determined to make a living by making things up. Upon graduation, he was hired as editor at large for an important Japanese magazine where he styled fashion shoots using colorful cellophane and tinsel and painted props like celestial ceilings with planets and angels. He was best known for his monthly column on any topic he fancied. He wrote that all the chickens, rabbits, roosters, etc., sold on the Right Bank near the Seine should be pets, not dinner. He wrote about the colors of light in Paris, the industrial neighborhoods, the aristocratic culture of tarnished silver at the flea markets, mother-of-pearl buttons, boxes and knife handles, and when he went to Egypt and saw the Nile he wrote about the colors of water around the world and about the djellabahs, gold earrings, scarabs and dead queens. He brought back djellabahs and gold earrings and patinated scarabs, but it was impossible to bring back a dead queen. Ishimoto was feeling disappointed with living humans, imperfect and insensitive to nuance. He began to think of dead queens day and night. In profile. In gold. In alabaster. In obsidian. When Ishimoto falls in love with the bust of an Egyptian woman he sees on a postcard from the Walters Art Gallery in Baltimore, he moves there to be with her, which is possible six days a week. The museum is closed on Monday. He also takes up the study of harpsichord at Peabody Music School and ancient Egyptian grammar at

ISHIMOTO'S
WARDROBE

pink wings

white wings, two pairs

silver wings

*black wings, tips sprayed
gold*

ballet slippers, black

loafers sprayed silver

flip-flops, rubber

six djellabahs

*beaded satin and tulle
wedding dress cut off at
the knee*

pink sequin top

*white cotton button-
down shirt (worn under
pink sequin top)*

*jeans, sprayed silver at
the cuffs*

silk kimono collection

*Salvation Army polyester
floral shirt with large
collar*

*three vintage button-
down shirts in Liberty of
London floral prints*

*two Liberty of London
floral ties*

Johns Hopkins University so he can write
love letters to his new muse. He rents studio space to create valentines to her: etchings, paintings, sculptures in shells, love
letters written on old engravings.

It is around this time that he stops
cutting his hair and begins to color it dirty
blond. This is not an aspiration to emulate
Marilyn Monroe, but Botticelli's Venus.
His essays for the Japanese magazine
become stranger and stranger. "We admire
that you have explored many nuances of an
Egyptian bust," writes his editor, "about
the expression in her eyes, the fantasy of
her life among the living, her jewelry collection, musical tastes and afterlife, which
you have led us to believe is eternal since
her soul was lighter than a feather, but we
would be much obliged if your observations were to take on a new direction."

But by then the Egyptian queen was
speaking to him. His hair grew and his
roots grew in and his fingernail polish
chipped. He stopped bathing, and the
Japanese magazine politely rejected his
articles. He made an origami crane with
the first eviction notice. But when he tried
to leave the museum with his love interest
he ended up, after a brief interview, at the
Phipps Clinic.

Ishimoto is much happier after his tenure at Phipps. Art therapy is part of the curriculum. He writes several articles for the Japanese magazine and when he is released eight months later, he buys a new wardrobe at the costume shop. He buys several sets of angel wings and wears them constantly. A prominent gallery in Baltimore is giving him a show of his love objects to a dead queen.

Ryan

Yoga instructor/general labor foreman

AGE: 53

ASTROLOGICAL SIGN: Libra

BORN: Lower East Side, Manhattan

CURRENT DWELLING: three-story brick house in Jersey City

FAVORITE BOOK: *The Seven Storey Mountain* by Thomas Merton

FAVORITE MUSIC: Bob Dylan; Bruce Springsteen; Osamu Kitajima

FAVORITE MOVIES: *The Manchurian Candidate; Edward Scissorhands*

FAVORITE FOODS: *agedofu*

FAVORITE DRINKS: green tea

MOTTO: Something Mother Teresa said— Give until it hurts.

Ryan experienced his first awakening as an altar boy; he felt a presence in the big church when he was alone. He had a particular affection for Saint Francis of Assisi, who was there in stained glass.

By his teens the saint was displaced by Jack Kerouac, Ginsberg's *Howl* and *Kaddish,* Ferlinghetti, soul music and Motown.

Drafted. After serving a year in Vietnam he moved to Newport Beach, lived with a surfer and a cat named José in a furnished beach house, his $300 1967 Plymouth Belvedere parked slapdash, half on the lawn out front. He was a Libra, peace was his mantra, but Vietnam lingered—the humid air, lethal leaves and a camaraderie of intimacy and shared soldier drama. Nothing here—not sun or ocean or warlessness—made him feel useful, so he wore his green army cap year-round and drank. He drank a lot. Beer, scotch, tequila, nobody could do more shots, and each day he did not wake up and drive someplace distant like Neal Cassady but just got up and drank black coffee until it was time for a real drink. When he finally sobered up, tai chi, body surfing and beach volleyball await-ed him, and a Zen master at a concrete company took him under his wing. Jackhammering concrete was his violently vibrating wake-up call, an affirmation that he could feel; operating tractors, forklifts, trucks and skip loaders—work became his prayer.

Ryan sold his "El Blanco Spector," which by then was held together inside by tape, and moved back to New York. He applied to the Peace Corps and lived in a boardinghouse in Brooklyn—a fireman in the basement, an iron worker on his floor and a con-struction worker upstairs. When the Peace Corps didn't pan out—harder to get into than the FBI, says Ryan—he got back into con-struction, but walking past a building on 13th Street on his way to a downtown job site he heard something, kirtan, early morning chants, faintly.

He started taking yoga in Manhattan; something about the place—chanting Om—resonated, evoked the stained-glass rever-ence and mysterious Latin chants he'd felt as an altar boy. He met a swami and started teacher training and eventually taught. Yoga level one. Yoga level two. Yoga level three. "We're all busy, compli-cated people," he tells his students. "Forget the story line." He reads *Yoga Journal* and tries out new poses on his students. Even inexpe-

rienced students feel strangely empow-
ered by his energy and give everything a
whirl.

Ryan buys a building but does not
think much about furniture. He has a meditation chair made of brown plastic, purchased at a thrift shop, a poster of Maria
Falconetti from *The Passion of Joan of Arc,*
the Carl Theodor Dreyer film, a large
peaceful Tibetan Buddha in plaster and a
few Hanuman pictures—he cannot
explain the affinity he feels for this monkey—scattered about. No pets to start
with until one of the strays he fed wan-
dered into the house one day and gave
birth in a closet. Ryan does not have e-mail
or a vehicle.

As a night foreman, currently gutting
sixteen floors of an office building in the
Fifties, Ryan feels metaphorically the satisfaction of the slate being wiped clean, of
clearing karma, of supreme emptiness,
filled with only the moment. And there is
the harmonizing of energies, of tasks being
performed together.

The gang of guys he supervises does
not take yoga classes. The guys call him
Dalai Lama and unwind at topless bars.
Before work on Thursdays, Ryan teaches a
yoga class. "I feel the way the student is
feeling," he says. "You feel like a beggar and

your bowl is empty when you go in, then you have this experience and your bowl is overflowing." At Christmas he brought all of his students Krishna lunch boxes. He has one left at home but does not bring it to the construction site.

overcoats in tweed, camel's-hair and cashmere from Star Struck, a vintage clothing store

thirty antique ties bought for the color or pattern; these are never worn

Atlas

Painter/writer/musician

AGE:	40
ASTROLOGICAL SIGN:	Taurus
BORN:	Leiden, the Netherlands
CURRENT DWELLING:	farmhouse in Gelderland, the Netherlands, near Zutphen
FAVORITE BOOKS:	*Candide* by Voltaire; *Eugene Onegin* by Aleksandr Pushkin; *The Hobbit* by J. R. R. Tolkien; *Jip en Jop in Mensenland* by Ank Wentink
FAVORITE MUSIC:	Haydn; Clara Rockmore on the theremin; anything with a sitar, including Ravi Shankar
FAVORITE MOVIES:	Toss-up between *The Wickerman,* original version, and *Valerie and Her Week of Wonders*
FAVORITE FOODS:	blood oranges; *gebraden haas* (roast hare)
FAVORITE DRINKS:	Anastasia blend tea by Kousmichoff; absinthe
MOTTO:	Create your own universe.

When Atlas was a boy, the human skulls and skeletons in his father's office at the university fascinated him. Things seemed promising for medical school until Atlas, twelve at the time, fainted during an autopsy. It became apparent that Atlas, who constantly carried around charcoal pencils and a sketch pad, was interested in anatomy only as it related to drawing. By the time he got into the Royal Academy of Fine Arts in Antwerp he was already an accomplished painter. His figures and interiors showed a sensitivity to light, atmosphere and texture that was evocative of Vermeer, and above his landscapes hovered cloud formations that were more expressive than Ruisdael's.

After graduating he took off for Russia, drank a lot of vodka, made a study of the architecture and learned how to play the balalaika. Next came India, where he learned to play the sitar and studied Sanskrit. He collected fabrics, carpets and lamps even though he had no place to put them. He painted postcards in watercolors and sent them to his grandmother in Gelderland. She had the portrait he did of her with her pet goat framed in gold and put in the living room. He painted it when he was thirteen.

When he returned to Holland he set up a studio on the top floor of a brick building along a canal in Amsterdam. He hung Indian fabrics and created a tentlike room to sleep in. He didn't have a bed, just carpets and pillows on the floor. He started every day with a pot of Russian tea and finished it with a glass or three of absinthe. To his surprise, his grandmother had kept all of his painted postcards and contacted a small gallery in the country that agreed to hold a show of Atlas' visual travelogue through Asia.

At twenty-five he was already gaining a reputation as an eccentric. After hours of painting he'd walk along the canals in a long claret-colored robe smoking a long clay pipe. He grew a beard and moustache and styled them in seventeenth-century fashion. He looked like the ghost of van Dyck. Tourists thought he was part of some historical reenactment troupe and clicked their cameras at him. Atlas never noticed, as he was always lost in thought, contem-

ATLAS' WARDROBE

*several full-length
embroidered silk robes*

kaftans from Morocco

*assorted tunics from
India in silk and cotton
in pastels, brights and
white*

*two eighteenth-century
banyans with covered
buttons*

Cossack blouse

*Russian peasant shirt in
unbleached muslin*

*several embroidered folk
shirts from the Ukraine*

*linen shirts with floppy
lace cuffs (he sews the
cuffs on himself)*

*waistcoats in striped
silk, damask and wool*

*Delft blue cashmere
turtleneck*

*two bulky wool cardigans
knitted by his grand-
mother*

*assorted scarves knitted
by his grandmother*

velveteen jackets

velvet beret

*assortment of straw hats
for painting* en plein air

Persian lamb hat

*black riding boots from
the Spanish Riding
School in Vienna*

plating his next painting, cloud formations
or the color of the sky.

Atlas is heartbroken when he learns
that his grandmother has died. She sup-
ported his dreams in life and now in death.
She leaves him her farmhouse, complete
with a painted Gypsy caravan, goats, cats,
Shetland pony, three geese, a dovecote and
pet weasels.

Packing up his oils and brushes and
bottles of turpentine and varnishes, Atlas
heads for the country. It is here that he has
lived for the last fifteen years. In this time
he has turned it into a fantastical mélange
of Near Eastern, Far Eastern, Gypsy and
Dutch décor. He leaves his doors open,
and the goats come and go as they please.
The geese cackle in the kitchen when they
want Atlas to feed them, and the weasels
sleep on a velvet cushion near the fireplace. In the summer, Atlas invites guests
to stay in the caravan. This is where he preferred to stay as a child when he visited his
grandmother. He has lined the interior
with velvets, damasks, fabrics with fringe
and tassels. Gold and silver thread sparkles
in the light of the lanterns that hang from
the ceiling.

He constructs miniature architectural
models of whimsical mansions and buildings with onion domes, turrets, atriums,

gables by the dozen, columns, flying but-
tresses. A German magazine is running a
feature on these. He is also working on his
first novel, handwritten in pen and ink.

Atlas' most profound relationships
are with his subjects: people who have
commissioned portraits or agreed to sit
for him. In the long hours observing
them—he never paints from photographs—he becomes intimate with their
every nuance, curve, gesture, coloration,
freckle and flush. He plays his harpsichord
for them, the sitar, a violin he has made
and decorated himself. On chilly days he
makes them *anijs melk* or cocoa. They
share, sometimes, even more than meals
and stories, but the relationship always
ends when the portrait is over.

Turkish slippers

*water buffalo sandals,
two pairs*

wooden shoes

indigo jeans, badly faded

*Prussian blue work
pants in heavy cotton
twill*

*velveteen jeans in purple
and black*

*red boiled-wool pants
with navy piping and
silver buttons*

*assorted shawls—he
shares these with his
harpsichord*

wool cape

black wool greatcoat

embroidered Afghan coat

raw linen nightshirts

Zouzou

Photographer/painter/photo gallery curator

AGE:	35
ASTROLOGICAL SIGN:	Pisces
BORN:	Vienna, Austria
CURRENT DWELLING:	Vienna, Austria
FAVORITE BOOKS:	Used to love Arthur Schnitzler. New favorites: *Eine Blassblaue Frauenschrift* by Franz Werfel; *Ungeduld des Herzens* by Stefan Zweig
FAVORITE MUSIC:	Johann Sebastian Bach, "especially *Goldbergvariationen,* the breathless version by Glenn Gould"; *Sketches of Spain* by Miles Davis; Portishead
FAVORITE MOVIES:	*À Bout du Souffle* by Jean-Luc Godard; *Fahrenheit 451* by François Truffaut; *The Cabinet of Dr. Caligari*
FAVORITE FOOD:	mousse au chocolat
FAVORITE DRINK:	heavy red French wine, unless it's Sturm season.
MOTTO:	*Der Weg ist das Ziel.* (The way is the goal.)

It's early November, and Zouzou's solo show is coming up in a few weeks. She picks up a bottle of Sturm on her way home from her day job at the Fotogalerie Wien where she has been putting together

Builder, the catalogue. Red wine is heavy, meditative, sexy, but Sturm is her favorite seasonal drink—it interests her because it's unfinished, in the process of becoming—a wine in the early stages of fermentation and sealed only with a cap of aluminum foil. She lifts the foil to smell the tangy, grapefruity odor. It's fleeting, like a blossom, short-lived like the flowers she paints and photographs intimately and abstractly: the stamen, a few petals unfurling, the space between petals. When people first see her work, they don't know what she has painted or photographed; orchids, roses and tulips up close metamorphose into lips, body parts, fetal curves, fiber-optic documents of a stomach's interior.

Wolfgang, her twenty-two-year-old live-in lover, is getting coal for the heater on his way home from art school. Zouzou is making dinner for American friends, a writer and a musician, and Americans are used to having heat. She has a painting studio near the photo gallery but does her printing at their home, an apartment on the fifth floor on Passauerplatz. The chemicals and enlarger are in the kitchen next to the olive oil, wine and sugar canister, which is filled with cubes and packets taken from cafés or *Konditorei*. Photo negatives are drying in the bathroom, which is where she cuts her hair. It is short, always a little uneven and tufted like a windblown thistle.

Zouzou and Wolfgang picked up the Americans at Hotel Graben their first night in Vienna and drove them around in Zouzou's rusted Citroën DS 19. Over Gluwein they decided to take them sightseeing. Zouzou suggested the Kunsthistorisches Museum, the Secession and the Schönbrunn Palace, but the Americans were more interested in undervisited, unpopular and subterranean places.

Zouzou had never been to the Bestattungsmuseum, but it was the first thing the Americans wanted to see. The tour guide rings a

*black jeans, five or six
pairs, from thrift shops.
These include Joop and
Diesel.*

assorted black sweaters

*turtlenecks in cotton,
wool and boiled wool, in
grey, black, navy and
white*

*large cable-knit and
thrift-shop cashmere
sweaters borrowed from
live-in boyfriend*

*long crushed-velvet skirt
in bottle green*

patchwork velvet skirt

Indian cotton skirt

*black silk Chinese jacket
with colorful embroidery
purchased in Hong Kong
on the occasion of her
photography exhibit*

*Vietnamese dress and
trousers in green and
red, purchased in Paris
on the occasion of her
photography show*

*fatigues from Soviet
army*

*black leather ballet flats
(she leaves these at the
painting studio)*

*Chinese brocade bedroom
slippers*

*black alligator high
heels, Ferragamo, from
thrift shop (worn twice)*

*black leather lace-up
boots*

little bell and explains to the group—
Zouzou, the Americans and a large couple
from Germany—that people used to be
buried with a string tied to their wrist that
led to a bell like this on the surface in case
there'd been a mistake and they should
happen to wake up. This haunts Zouzou as
they peruse things in the nearby thrift shop
after the tour. The musician buys a traditional Tyrolean jacket with horn buttons,
the writer, vintage garter belts and pieces
of memorial folk art. Zouzou finds a silver-plate candelabrum at least a hundred
years old and wonders if the owner was
buried alive. She had never considered that
the things she bought at thrift shops could
have belonged to dead people. She buys it
along with a few items for her opening—
a black sequin top to go with her black
jeans and a barely used bottle of Guerlain's
Jardins de Bagatelle.

She takes the Americans to visit the
burial sites of the Hapsburgs, all three
locations: coffins in one place, entrails in
another and hearts in a third. They pick up
Wolfgang after class and drive to
Zentralfriedhof cemetery where Wolfgang
and the musician root through the recently bulldozed dirt in the old part of the
cemetery and find pieces of bone: a skull
fragment, a rib, a vertebra and coffin han-

dles, while Zouzou photographs the young forest that has sprung up around the monuments and gravestones. It is like a set design, a scene from a nightmarish fairy tale. There are no flowers.

At dinner, Wolfgang recklessly throws on the coal. The Austrians feel toasty but the American writer gets up from the table during the salad and puts on her sweater. A little later, her hat.

"How can you paint flowers when you have all this great material around you?" asks the writer. "Skulls and bones and Hapsburg body parts in silver canopic jars like strange little jam pots. You have an endless supply of native Viennese resources here," she insists. Zouzou holds up an edible flower from the salad.

"Maybe I should have used some little chicken hearts and bones instead of flowers," she laughs.

There was a faint snow when they visited the carnival grounds early one evening on the outskirts of the city. The season was over, the rides were closed, buildings boarded up, and only one booth remained open. An old man huddled inside. Zouzou and Wolfgang bought Gitanes, and the musician bought a package of postcards of naked girls holding electric guitars to give to the guys in his

black ankle boots

Chinese brocade platform shoes from the forties (special occasions only)

black leather full-length coat

parka, vintage military issue

rabbit fur hat

pink-and-grey tweed coat with large pink buttons

striped cotton T-shirts in navy and white

coarse natural linen nightshirt from the marché aux puces *at Porte de Clignancourt*

assorted gloves, one pair fingerless

band. The musician asks Zouzou if she ever paints nudes and she says, "All my flowers are naked, they are not shy and show me everything." She can't help but see her Vienna in a new light, and she photographs the empty Ferris wheel looking like a black skeleton against a snow-bleak sky, and the broken ribs of an old wooden fence. Tomorrow they will visit the catacombs beneath St. Stephansdom and she will bring her camera even though it's not allowed.

Long after the Americans are gone, Zouzou receives a grant for a new collection of work: underground Vienna—bells and bones.

VI
BOHEMIAN
MISCELLANEA

BOHEMIAN ASTROLOGY

Aries

Reckless. Impulsive. Independent. Aries Bohemians like to break rules, but in more overt ways than other signs. Artistic rules. Grammatical rules. Dress-code rules. Postal rules. They send letters with "creative," i.e., vague addresses and in nonregulation-size envelopes that are too large or too small. They apply stamps on a tilt or in the middle of the envelope. Sometimes they have no patience for mail at all and they just show up.

Aries Bohemians will buy a cool vintage car on impulse and drive away on a whim. Gregarious and manic, they will talk at least one other person, possibly an Aquarius, Sagittarius or drifty Pisces into the road trip, destination to be decided on the road.

They are the sign most likely not to get the "required" immunization for remote travel and may forget their identification for domestic flights. Not without persuasive power, they have been known to talk their way onto the plane anyway. It's either that or a huge argument. They have a problem with this whole invasion of privacy thing and aren't shy about speaking up for their rights. Aries Bohemians may also be incredibly soft-spoken, to override a natural tendency toward volume.

They like to put on a show. A magic show, for example. They may be enamored of science fiction and monuments, time machines and Stonehenge, big things and big ideas.

No sign has more big ideas than Aries. Aries gets high on ideas. Aries would love to think up ideas all day. But despite the fact they are the number one fire sign, Aries have a hard time with execution, and so are always off to a new idea, a new conquest, a new high. Too cerebral? A head case? They squeeze paint straight from the tube and get to work. Who needs art school or a gallery? It's about passion, the immediate gratification.

It's good for Aries to have a practical type around to help them jettison their ideas into the world. When they do have a job, whether it's a show of their work, a play or a review to write, they wait until the last minute to meet the deadline. They like the rush.

Taurus

The Taurus Bohemian is not usually the one squatting in an abandoned building, but should you find one who is, the place will be cozy. Cushions, overstuffed chairs, carpets, art on the walls, candles and decent wine. The Taurus Bohemian might create an intimate space by hanging fabric remnants. Even if these were found in a Dumpster on Canal Street in New York, the decorations will create warmth once the creature-comfort-loving Taurus has installed them. Taurus Bohemians will find a couch on the street and reupholster it themselves. Never mind that they have no training in upholstery. They're hands-on. Very hands-on. They are physically demonstrative and more indulgent of the senses than any other Bohemian. Their ideal day would start with waking up when they feel like it, making love, sipping an espresso and eating caviar and scrambled eggs, making love, napping, drinking red wine, making music and making love, lighting the hash pipe, taking a nap, and so forth and so on.

Taurus Bohemians are one of the most musically gifted signs, and there will be at least one musical instrument in the Taurus habitat. They are so musically gifted they can create music out of anything, even a typewriter, like Erik Satie. They usually cook, too. Even if they have a simple hot plate, they can cook up pasta Bolognese. It was Taurean Salvador Dalí, after all, who wrote a cookbook. One last thing to note: The Taurus is patient. When Taurus Bohemians get an idea, watch out. They are relentless. Once they have decided to do something, whether it's opening a pottery shop or supporting a cause, they're unbudgeable. They are able to think through an idea slowly and analytically and believe profoundly in the power of such thoughts. Think Karl Marx.

Gemini

Wanderlust supreme. Mind games. Multitalented. Gemini Bohemians can't bear being pinned down to one thing. They could direct, cast, write and act in their own film, not as a control issue but simply because they can. The sound track, too? Quite possibly. They may study one thing, but even if they stick to it, they'll dabble in other universes and magically combine seemingly disparate elements.

They are the most spiritually restless, seeking universal consciousness and perfection in alternative religions and foreign geography. It was Gemini Allen Ginsberg who helped popularize the meditative Sanskrit word *om* in the United States.

You will most likely meet them en route. On a train. By a pyramid, in the Andes, by the sea, in a hotel lobby, in Père-Lachaise, in a temple in Nepal. They are stimulated by everything and crave stimulation and will happily go on adventures with you. They are the Bohemians who say, Cairo on June 22? I'll be there. Le Pont Neuf at three? No problem. Casablanca tomorrow? Which café?

They are able to translate the cryptic, the detailed and the personal into a universal language. They may also be cryptic and personal, leaving you a note at your hotel that reads: *Aussi loin que le vent le dit.* Good luck.

Their specialty is communication. Geminis have many strange ideas to convey through theater, video art, songs, philosophy, prose, poems or images. Even when they are not writers, you will feel a strange compulsion to save all their letters, or even their e-mails. They are very seductive, the most flirtatious of all Bohemians. Ever curious, they are the ones most likely to read up on tantric sex. Sleeping with a Gemini is like having a ménage à trois.

Cancer

Don't expect to read one line of a Cancer's novel until it's done or glimpse the painting until the final stroke. Cancer Bohemians excel at the solitary arts. Privacy is one operative word. Homebody is the other. While other Bohemians may pick up and move when the rent is overdue, Cancer Bohemians will take all kinds of odd jobs in order not to be evicted. They are the touring band member who can't wait to get back home, the painter with a show in Paris who can't wait to get back home. The novelist who wants to experience

Timbuktu but can't wait . . . They are far more comfortable with astral traveling.

Cancer Bohemians are highly intuitive. They make great mediums, psychics, tarot and palm readers, and because they can easily learn to read an ephemeris, astrologer is another profession to which they may gravitate. It is for this reason that Cancer Bohemians will take this with a grain of salt. They consider far more than the sun sign. Where is the moon? The ascendant? The angles and houses? This is just the icing. Where's the cake?

Cancers also like old things. They have an eye for them and can instinctively intuit the value. Other people may walk right by a Georgian silver ladle, but the Cancer picks it right up. While no Bohemian wants mass-market merchandise in their home, Cancers find it particularly repellent. Cancer Bohemians do not trust "progress" and "technology," and they will be the ones in full swing during the blackout. They have a Victrola, manual typewriter, quill pens, dial phone and an emergency radio, the kind you crank. They're prepared.

It's safe to say they are always a little worried, and have we mentioned private? They actually believe Big Brother is watching. No EZ Pass or navigation systems in their vehicles. They don't want their movements monitored.

Leo

That dashing fellow in the cape and top hat at the New Year's Eve party is a Leo. Leo Bohemians vibrate with creative intensity. You can feel them in the room, and they expect you to. They like the limelight, being onstage. Please, go ahead, praise their last *Hamlet,* jazz riff, book, article or pas de deux. Ask for an autograph. But the praise should be specific; they're really listening when it's all about them. Leo Bohemians have no interest in rules unless they've made them up. They host literary salons with style and confidence. If the electricity is turned off, for example, the Leo Bohemian is never flustered but brings out all the candles and makes the ambience seem deliberate. Microphone not working? On with the show.

Leo Bohemians are unflustered by large groups and enjoy organizing others. A theater company? Commune? Animal sanctuary? Cross-country caravan? Everybody wants to hop on the Leo bandwagon. They make it work. They are particularly creative with children's theater. This does not mean that they are bombastic, loud or overbearing. Leo Bohemians lead majestically, with an air of nobility, graciousness and generosity. If you should find yourself in dire straits, seek the Leo; they will always help. Just remember to thank them profusely. For years.

Leos want to fix things, run things and direct. They want to lead new movements and create change. They have unorthodox ideas about how to work with "mental patients," and they excel at psychodrama. No matter what they do for a living, even if it's bartending, they do it with a flourish. Anything they do becomes a dramatic art.

Virgo

The idea of a Bohemian Virgo would seem at first to be somewhat of a paradox. The typical equation is Virgo neat, Bohemian dirty. The Virgo, unafflicted, is the cleanest of Bohemians, especially when it comes to hygiene. They are not slothful, either. This Bohemian, unless on a night shift, gets up earlier than any other Bohemian. Blame the stars.

Virgo Bohemians nevertheless are hardly mainstream. They are practitioners of alternative and fringe medicine, study midwifery and Mayan abdominal massage, shiatsu, the Alexander technique and herbology. They may find their niche in organic farming and are great in the garden—they will know all the Latin names—and all plants thrive under their care, even poisonous plants, for which they have a mysterious affinity. They may grow poppies, foxglove, jimsonweed, wolfsbane and other varieties of unconsumable plants or cultivate a garden that's strictly purple or thorny. There will always be some strange quirk to Virgo gardens no matter how wholesome they purport to be. You can trust them, however, to tell you exactly which Bach Flower Remedy, tea or herb you need to take whether you're suffering from a serious ailment or are simply under the weather.

They may also be able to fix your radio, recalibrate your odometer, tune up your Vespa and tune your piano.

Virgo Bohemians may tend sheep and goats, weave, tie-dye, embroider (no sign is better at details), blow glass, work in clay, tool leather, or make jewelry and furniture, dream catchers, stained glass and violins.

Virgo Bohemians also excel at the technical aspects of the arts. Web design, for example. (They will even have a contract for you to sign.) They like photography, and they always have their own darkroom. They are not very organized, however, and may not be able to find negatives when you want a print of that photograph of the ossuary they shot in Prague.

Libra

Libra Bohemians are all for shacking up. They can't bear to be alone, and they are happiest in a society of like-minded Bohemians. They love to be part of salons, troupes, bands, new group enterprises. They excel at parties, whether it's being a guest or hosting them, but they prefer to be the guest; they get to dress up, eat, drink and be charming without any of the work. Libra is, after all, the most charming sign and therefore is always on the party guest list.

Libras want Peace, Love and Understanding. John Lennon's song "Imagine" epitomizes the Libra quest for a harmonious world. This does not mean, however, that they are uninterested in superficial things, like fashion. No one is more inventive with style than Libras. They are, to be fair, often as stylish with words as they are with fabric (noted examples include Truman Capote, Gore Vidal and Oscar Wilde), but it is with materials that Libra is in full swing. Libra Bohemians like to rip apart, sew on embroidery or fuzzy trim, change buttons and add cuffs, drape Indian fabrics, toiles or velvets over the windows, window boxes, lamps and chairs. They are not offended, unless they are PETA types, by your gift of old fur collars cleaned out of your grandmother's attic. They envision fur trim on all their sweaters and coats. (Libra artist Meret Oppenheim even fur-trimmed a teacup, saucer and spoon and called it *Breakfast in Fur.*)

Libra Bohemians haunt thrift shops, flea markets, sample sales and attics but are unlikely to be found sorting through anything that's grimy—too offensive—or truly disorganized. They're too lazy.

Libra Bohemians often have more than one talent and can't decide which path to follow. Singing? Aromatherapy? Mural painting? Photography? Graphic design? Acting? They may be adept at and dabble in them all when not napping or indulging in fine wine and food. (They share the planet Venus with Taurus.) Libra Bohemians always manage a peaceful atmosphere and get dressed up for every meal. Breakfast in bed might warrant a vintage kimono, smoking jacket or dressing gown. The outfit for dinner might be *chinois* for Chinese takeout or tweed and tartan for haggis or shepherd's pie. Libras, like all Bohemians, like to be naked. They adore the arts as much as they adore the idea of being a muse, which makes the profession of nude modeling ideal.

Scorpio

Scorpio Bohemians go all the way. They are the most intensely determined of all the signs, the least capable of moderation. To Dylan Thomas, for example, life was poetry without compromise, drinking without limits. Scorpios also like to get their way. Picasso, who was not tall, rich or handsome, got a date with any girl he fancied through the sheer potency of his will. It's an honor to be a muse to the Scorpio.

No other Bohemians have better follow-through once they have a worthwhile project. Even if Scorpios wake up at noon, you can bet they'll be pursuing these personal goals until the sun sets, interrupted only by interludes with a bedfellow. The acts of creation and procreation are regenerating to the Scorpio. Don't ever ask them to change something in a dance piece, script or painting. Just don't.

Scorpio Bohemians are at ease with the concept of death and regeneration; Pluto, lord of the underworld, is their guide. Scorpios are the ones putting up the black drapes, buying a vintage hearse for their band to gig and drinking wine out of a human skull. They are the ones with the taxidermy bats and a worn volume of *The Tibetan Book of the Dead*. They see no shame in the functions of the human body, and Scorpios in the health field may make a living doing colonics.

The reproductive organs are also of great interest to Scorpios. You'll most likely find a print of an erotic Japanese woodcut, and a large portion of their reading material may be devoted to erotica.

It is rumored that you have not had sex until you've had sex with a Scorpio. Scorpios just shrug when they hear this. Shrug and smile.

Sagittarius

This is the sign that's built for the road, whether it's literal travel, or the road to higher consciousness. Sagittarius Bohemians on an intellectual or spiritual quest may live Spartan-style, with little more than a crate of books, a coffeepot and a yoga mat. When they do have a room, it's got to have a view; no basement sublet for these Bohemians, they'd rather live in a tree house. But even this type likes to get up and go. They view restlessness as a positive attribute. The Sagittarius might fly to India to meet a guru and learn about Hinduism and Sanskrit and end up staying a year. They love new cultures that seem more colorful and chaotic than the ones they're from. They may travel a great distance to see a butterfly migration, manatees or the aurora borealis. They are the philosophers of the zodiac, the seekers of truth, liberty and higher learning. They have a strong need to express themselves creatively, and their work is highly imaginative and individualistic. Check out the mystical work of poet William Blake or the underlit demimonde paintings of Toulouse-Lautrec.

But don't let all this higher learning stuff fool you. Sagittarius Bohemians are famous for having a great capacity to party. When they drink, they can drink you under the table. Blame it on their lust for life.

It is hard to pin down Sagittarius Bohemians. They are not likely to believe in the institution of marriage, and the idea of monogamy is mysterious to them. Lovers in several cities are a distinct possibility. They will never ask you how many lovers you have, and they expect the same courtesy.

Capricorn

This sign was always "my way or the highway," but with a Bohemian, it's even worse. Capricorn Bohemians are more stubborn than Taurus Bohemians and are secretly so fragile that they make up for it with an inflated sense of self. They are the ultimate paranoids. They do not trust the corporate world with their inventions, music or ideas and put a big-circled copyright © on anything they touch and have considered using it on postcards. They're cautious discussing their projects, and it's not uncommon to hear resentful lamentations such as "They stole my idea" and "They copied my style" or "Next time I'm directing it myself."

They often turn down opportunities where they feel they will lose creative control or have to share their profits. Why should an agent or dealer get a percent or share of royalties? They are the artists, after all. No agent is ever good enough for Capricorn Bohemians, and for this reason their strange and immense talent often goes unrecognized or doesn't rise above a certain plateau.

Capricorn Bohemians brood over every decision and have an excellent work ethic—as long as it's their work. You won't catch them doing your typing unless they have an ulterior motive. Because they are so critical, they are the do-it-yourself type. They make their own films and self-publish. They actually enjoy their own company more than any other sign, and they excel at being alone. Their negativity and darkness gives them insights into creating extreme art, and no sign can better write about isolation and disappointment. After their demise, many works of genius, from orchestral compositions to plays, may be found in drawers, desks and boxes that they were too paranoid to submit lest the work be misunderstood, rejected, stolen or plagiarized.

Because they like to be in control, Capricorns may also read tarot cards, do astrology charts, become chiropractors. Their favorite color: black. It should be noted that they have an excellent sense of humor. It is of the dry variety.

Aquarius

They want a better world, and they think it starts with you.

They will tell you that you've dropped something or littered. They will tell you that your car is idling and giving children asthma. They will go into buildings in search of the person leaving the car idling. Aquarius Bohemians may be activists. They may even strap themselves to vessels to prevent whaling or live in a two-hundred-foot redwood tree to save it. They take in stray animals, the more undesirable and strange the better, and make discoveries that they fancy will help the environment, humankind or animal kind. Ask the Aquarius Bohemian to solve a problem and the answer will be out of this world. Aquarius Bohemians may, in fact, do any number of oddball things: write an astrology column, teach workshops in Kotodama or the kabbalah as sacred psychology, create mobiles of old silver-plate spoons, play the theremin or paint electrical storms. Aquarius Bohemians love to shock for the sake of shocking. They do this with no apparent effort.

Aquarius in love? Don't expect roses. They will write an ode to you, curl it into a bottle and release it in the river Tweed, the Seine, the Hudson or the Nile. If you're lucky, they'll deliver it to your doorstep. They will bring you oysters in a snowstorm, knit you a cap, sew you a cape with strange frogs. Better give them a lot of room, however, or their love knit unravels.

Aquarius Bohemians embrace electronic gizmos and technology. They are the most progressive of Bohemians, but since they are also the most eccentric they may shun television and carry on about its brainwashing powers and project Super-8 films on the garden wall. Cars may be out of the question as well—they ruin the environment. Many Aquarians travel by bicycle.

Pisces

Pisces is the most misunderstood and poetic sign, and the Pisces Bohemian is an enigma. With a cavalier attitude toward timetables, they have to muster all their willpower to be prompt. The Pisces sense of time is vaporous, ethereal. If you look closely at their antique pocket watch or wristwatch you will see that it's purely decorative. They may have even had it repaired once but blame their particular type of energy field for the watch stopping.

Pisces Bohemians may have strange collections of things. They might own fifty pairs of shoes, forty-five hats and twenty-five teapots but have only two spoons. Go figure.

Pisces may lack skills others take for granted, such as driving, since there may be confusion between brake and gas after long non-driving intervals; besides, they daydream, so it's really best not to have them behind the wheel. On the road, or in the coffee shop, they will be soaking up the atmosphere and the conversation, quietly absorbing it all to later document in memoir, fiction, poetry, art or dance. Pisces Bohemians create true alternative work simply by expressing themselves, which may be a nebulous, little-understood world, even to them. Pisces Bohemians are the most deeply spiritual of all the Bohemians, even if they do not actively practice a formal religion. George Harrison never got over his trip to India with the Beatles; it shaped his music for the rest of his life.

Pisces Bohemians do not show any overt signs of ambition and may be considered lazy—they sleep and therefore dream more than any other sign—and it's always amazing to see what they can accomplish with no apparent fanfare. Lou Reed, called lazy by Andy Warhol, wrote a song with the lyrics, "I am a lazy son, I never get things done."

Formality of any sort is often anathema to Pisces, who drift in and out of the conscious realm with apparent ease. This is annoying to many people, especially authority figures. Pisces Bohemians in the arts need a great deal of nurturing and encouragement, as they are not very well adapted to coping with the corporate world or the material plane. Heaven help you when they get depressed.

They are the messiest of all Bohemians.

Everything you've heard about Pisces and addiction is true.

THE BOHEMIAN QUIZ

WHAT KIND of BOHEMIAN ARE YOU:
WELL-ROUNDED, SPLIT PERSONALITY
or a DEFINITE TYPE?

1. Your dentist says you need a root canal and it will be quite expensive. You . . .

    a. offer to play music, juggle or draw caricatures at your dentist's son's bar mitzvah.

    b. go through several bottles of Ambesol until the tooth falls out.

    c. make monthly visits to the dentist for cleaning, etc., so dental overhauls are not necessary.

    d. tell the dentist that you're sure your toxic old fillings are your real problem, but since the planet Mercury is in retrograde it's not a good time to start.

    e. offer to redecorate the waiting room.

2. You're on a road trip with friends and have run out of food money. You . . .

    a. help yourself to nature's bounty—fruit from an orchard, corn from a field, etc.

    b. pawn your guitar, great-uncle's pocket watch, etc., in the nearest town.

    c. work at a soup kitchen or local ashram in return for food.

    d. polish off what's left in the flask and keep driving until you get to a fine restaurant where you order the most expensive entrée on the menu and the finest Champagne. Then thank the waiter for a lovely meal and impeccable service and make your exit, acting as though you've left cash and a handsome tip in the billfold.

    e. would never let this happen, so you pay for everyone.

3. Driving with friends, you're pulled over for speeding and have no driver's license. You . . .

    a. hide the pot and give the officer your friend's license.

    b. tell the officer you've had quite a hectic day at country auctions and to please, please pick something out of the back of the vehicle and forget about this silly thing.

    c. if the vehicle is "borrowed," wait until the officer gets out of the car and approaches you and then floor it.

    d. ask the officer where you can get a pair of those cool boots.

    e. start chanting.

4.   You're about to be evicted for
     nonpayment of rent. You . . .

     a. call your dealer, publisher, aunt,
        great-aunt, anyone, everyone, for an
        "advance," because you can't bear to
        move all your stuff again.
     b. are packed up before the notice
        even arrives.
     c. hold a rent party.
     d. think, No problem. By the time this
        goes to court you'll be in Tibet.
     e. must have forgotten when you were
   making that documentary film in the Middle East
for a few months.

5.   You move from Portland, Maine, to New York City to paint
     for a month and discover a rat in your basement studio.
     You . . .

     a. a basement studio? Are you kidding? This would never
        happen. No, thank you.
     b. move your sleeping bag to your worktable.
     c. feed it, get it a running wheel and learn to live together.
     d. figure you must be hallucinating and pay it no mind.
     e. think, How exciting, I must be in New York. This
        experience can only enhance your creativity, and you start
        to keep a journal.

6.   It's 7:30 in the morning and the bell rings. You . . .

     a. assume it's the police or the landlord and don't answer.
     b. get out of bed and answer the door in the nude.
     c. are still meditating, and think, life is all about tests, and
        decide to let it go.

  d. put on a smoking jacket or kimono, take a quick glance in
     the mirror and run hands through hair before answering.

  e. think what a mistake it was to have booked a shiatsu
     appointment when you were at a party till 5:00 a.m.

7. You're feeling depressed. You . . .

  a. take advantage of the angst and paint a tortured
     self-portrait.

  b. play melodramatic music, e.g., Jean Sibelius' *Finlandia*
     and Gustav Mahler's *Das Lied von der Erde,* and systemically
     drain all the decanters.

  c. drink the leftover red wine, get the razor blade and
     scissors and dramatically alter your appearance in the
     bathroom mirror.

  d. forget tofu and brown rice. Hello, fast food and
     chocolate!

  e. struggle between rescuing animals at the shelter and a
     shopping spree at Christie's Oriental erotic art auction.

8. Your vehicle overheats and you find yourself next to a lake.
    You . . .

  a. go skinny-dipping, play a little music and maybe camp out
     there for the night.

  b. realize there are no mistakes and decide to listen to the
     cicadas and watch the bullrushes wave rhythmically in the
     wind until the car cools.

  c. get water from the lake for the radiator and get back on
     the road, for chrissake!

  d. seek the most majestic house on the lake and ask for
     coolant for the vehicle and rye for your flask.

  e. enjoy the smoked salmon, open the Pouilly Fumé, and
     wait for road service.

9.   You can't sleep. You . . .

   a. drink some red wine, smoke some hash and sketch the
       person sleeping in your bed.

   b. fire up a pot of coffee and rehearse your monologue
       loudly enough to wake up your roommate so you have
       someone to talk to. If you do not have a monologue, get
       out the typewriter or play your guitar.

   c. light some incense, put on a CD of *The Eternal Music of
       Nature* and go online to check out airfares to all your
       dream destinations from India to the Himalayas.

   d. start polishing the silver plate you picked up at the flea
       market. That's bound to put you to sleep.

   e. call other proven insomniacs and invite them out for
       drinks. Either that or finally start your memoirs.

10. You're at a new job and you get a call that you have to be at
     an audition in an hour. You . . .

   a. say nothing and vanish.

   b. photocopy a hundred of your résumés, poems, etc., then
       tell your manager your father is dying and you have to go
       to the hospital.

   c. disable your screen saver, position a full cup of chai on
       your desk, rub your laughing Buddha and trust in the
       universe that no one will notice your absence.

   d. tell your boss you feel an "onset of the spleen" and need
       to see your physician at once.

   e. request a leave of absence for the rest of the day. If
       questioned or denied, resign.

11. Your idea of breakfast is . . .

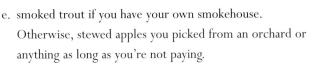

   a. leftover caviar, poached eggs, crêpes
      Suzette.

   b. coffee and a cigarette.

   c. ProGreens or Hawaiian spirulina
      with filtered water followed by
      leftover brown rice with
      soymilk, cinnamon and nutmeg.

   d. tin of smoked oysters and a pot of
      Lapsang Souchong. Simple toast, two-
      day-old brioche or old fortune
      cookies as available.

   e. smoked trout if you have your own smokehouse.
      Otherwise, stewed apples you picked from an orchard or
      anything as long as you're not paying.

ANSWERS:

1. a, Gypsy; b, Beat; c, Nouveau; d, Zen; e, Dandy
2. a, Gypsy; b, Beat; c, Zen; d, Dandy; e, Nouveau
3. a, Beat; b, Dandy; c, Gypsy; d, Nouveau; e, Zen
4. a, Dandy; b, Gypsy; c, Beat; d, Zen; e, Nouveau
5. a, Dandy; b, Beat; c, Zen; d, Gypsy; e, Nouveau
6. a, Gypsy; b, Beat; c, Zen; d, Dandy; e, Nouveau
7. a, Beat; b, Dandy; c, Gypsy; d, Zen; e, Nouveau
8. a, Gypsy; b, Zen; c, Beat; d, Dandy; e, Nouveau
9. a, Gypsy; b, Beat; c, Zen; d, Dandy; e, Nouveau
10. a, Gypsy; b, Beat; c, Zen; d, Dandy; e, Nouveau
11. a, Nouveau; b, Beat; c, Zen; d, Dandy; e, Gypsy

ACKNOWLEDGMENTS

I am profoundly grateful to my cowriters: Paul Gregory Himmelein, who read aloud to me *On the Road* and the whole of William Makepeace Thackeray's *The Paris Sketch Book* and who knows enough about coffee to write its history. He's my favorite kind of Bohemian, a Dandy, and proves you don't need money to look dapper—see the twenty-four-hour starving artist diet based on his early days in Manhattan.

And Patrisha Robertson, for perfuming pages with her patchouli sensibility, for sharing her spiritual views on animals, nudity, names and cinema; her every note is a Bohemian poem or manifesto, her dreamy Aquarian-electric life an inspiration. When a stranger asked, "Do you work for personal ambition or money?" Patrisha said, "I work for dreams."

I am grateful to Jill Cohen, a publisher who melds Scorpio instinct with intellect; Betty Wong, my dream editor—patient, thorough—her insights like whispers from my subconscious, only a lot more logical.

A deep, resonant, velvety thanks to Carly Sommerstein for lending me her Bohemian library (how many people do you know who have not one but two copies of *The Alice B. Toklas Cook Book, New American Writing* and an American book of slang lying around the house?), for smoothing the bumps of my sentences while amping up the color and for sashaying up to Norman Mailer and kissing him on the cheek.

Anna Jardine, mermaid of Carmine Street, for sharing books on splendor and squalor and editing brilliantly, unsparingly and severely an early draft.

Kimberly Forrest for reading the final draft with a golden pencil and advising with comments like "You need a splendor count" and "You can only use *gambol* once in a book"; Karim Sai for the sound of sand in Luxor at moonlight, the *septième silence* and the *septième sens;* Donna Brodie for saintly sensitivity and leonine generosity and of course the strange kingdom over which she presides, The Writers Room.

For inspiration and stories:

Thea Osato (goddess of Baltimore with salons and stories galore)

Nick Ghiz (who deserves a manual all his own)

Russell Joseph Buckingham (for the slightly shredded Victorian fan, *Ruggles of Red Gap* and Charlemagne's fur)

Les Hangad (the real McCoy, the ultimate muse, even has a "Paris" neon light in his Brooklyn studio, which he's heating by candlelight until he installs the boiler, and of course he built his own tub). Threads of Les are woven throughout this book; I am grateful to him, too, for sharing the particulars of his wedding-in-Woodstock outfit.

Kitty Lorentzen (for spiritual splendor)

Liam in Ireland

Liz Dougherty Pierce

Ira Cohen

The Metzlers: Kiki, Eric, Leif, Karl and Zora

Karen Sledge

Donald Blumberg and Christine Blumberg

Greg Day

Erica Danfield Cole (our lady of the ribbons)

Cody Melville

Tim Ryan (for heart lessons)

Vanessa Sanchez (for her voluptuous compassion, tenderness, candor, humor and Va-Va-Om)

Robin Bergland of Nantucket (for the Notre-Dame wedding)

Sara Bengur (We had to catch up on three-and-a-half-thousand years, after all.)

Eve

Susi Gamauf (for Viennese splendor)

Achim Hölzle

Larry J. Ruhl and Jeff Serouya of High Falls Mercantile for Dandy splendor

Julie Bleha

Alina Moscovitz

Eric Shaw

Ellen Kinnally

Jonathan Marder

Lorri Sendel and Mats Hakansson (for sharing their angel-love wedding)

Barry del Sherman

Izak, heartful, soulful, giant-eyed artist of this book, who cooked me a comforting breakfast on a snowy day and who, in true

Bohemian style, is terribly late and creating voluptuous paintings with colors flown in from Paris as I write this; Christy Fletcher for her sensitivity and patience and for finding this book its perfect home; Michael Carlisle for being both the perfect businessman and perfect gentleman; Ron Taft for magnificent, stellar professional counsel and for making all the stars align harmoniously; Justine for ironing out the kinks and making things flow; Diana Howard, for her intimate visual understanding of this book and for making room for me on her magic carpet during the journey; Kenny Ross (my Bombshell web designer) for expertise in music and all kinds of Bohemian opinions; Marion Ettlinger for enchantment and poetry; T.R., the one and only Snake Boy, my Sandman, for opening Bohemian gateways; Elizabeth Ennis, Virgo muse, for going through her library and suggesting films; Naked Angels Theatre for giving me the opportunity to hear my work in progress; special thanks to Kenneth Lonergan for making even dry asylum footnotes funny; Randall Ryan for driving us all off the road and giving wondrous buzz to the Zen Bohemian; Tim Ransom for reading Percy to perfection; Liz Benjamin, for big-hearted introductions; Stephanie Cannon for interpreting *Bohemian Manifesto* with sensitivity and electricity and especially for how she read "Dust"; Joe Danisi, creative director of Tuesdays @ Nine for chivalry, showmanship and magnetic readings; Jacques Boulanger of Creative Audio Post for narrative wizardry; Master Nan Lu for the gift of qi and inexplicable riddles; Dr. Mingxia Li for getting to the root of the monkey patch; Dr. Mitchell Gaynor for singing crystal bowls; Christine Nolin; Julianna Rizzo; Frances Hathaway and Deirdre Sullivan for lavender, illuminations and ethereal makeup for all my events; Rick Marin for taking the creases out of my introduction; James Rowe for trumpet-toned absinthe recipes and for compelling me to run out and buy novels by Bohumil Hrabal; Joseph

Alfieris for publishing "Dust" with light-strewn enchantment in *Contents;* Matthew Parr for the brilliant, strange and authoritative handmade cover type font in tarnished gold created for my proposal; Jeffrey Jeppesen for articulating my Bohemian desires and for composure during the perpetual avalanches of my books; Tobias Cox and all my friends at Three Lives Bookstore for career counseling; Patrick Malloy at Barnes and Noble for magnanimous magic; John Demsey for Bohemian brainstorming and the Truffaut filmstrip concept; James Gager for teaching me to use a heavy black pen with precision and levity; Maman, also known as mommy-o, for fielding questions on everything from jazz to grammar. Most of all, I would like to thank Sakti Narayani Amma.

The Writers

Laren Stover is the author of *The Bombshell Manual of Style* and *Pluto, Animal Lover,* dramatically adapted for Naked Angels' works-in-progress. She lives in a fourth-floor walk-up in Greenwich Village and is a member of The Writers Room.

Paul Gregory Himmelein sketched his first nude model at the age of three. In college he studied fine arts and art history. Since then, he has been in several bands and exhibited at various galleries. He is a member of The Writers Room, where he is working on his first novel.

Patrisha Robertson is a textsmith/knitter who lives in Toronto with her Scottie, Hamish. Formerly an editor, PR consultant and journalist, she now has her own company, Girl's Own! She has written one book for children and likes to think in rhyme.

The Illustrator

A rarity in a pixelated, digital world, Parisian-born Izak creates fluid, willowy watercolors in his downtown New York atelier. His illustrations charm the pages of *Vogue, Elle, In Style, The New York Times Magazine, Condé Nast Traveler, Sposa* and *Town & Country* and bring the images of major fashion and beauty companies to life. His books include *Princess, You Know Who You Are, Cooking for Mr. Latte* and *Essentially Lilly: A Guide to Colorful Entertaining.* Izak is represented by Traffic in New York.

The author invites you to visit www.bohemianmanifesto.com.